For Robert

LAKESIDE
RAMBLINGS

LAKESIDE RAMBLINGS

A year's walks and encounters at Stanwick Lakes

BOB GOTCH

The Book Guild Ltd

First published in Great Britain in 2017 by
The Book Guild Ltd
9 Priory Business Park
Wistow Road, Kibworth
Leicestershire, LE8 0RX
Freephone: 0800 999 2982
www.bookguild.co.uk
Email: info@bookguild.co.uk
Twitter: @bookguild

Typeset in Minion Pro

Printed and bound in Great Britain by CPI Group (UK) Ltd, Croydon, CR0 4YY

ISBN 978 1912083 152

British Library Cataloguing in Publication Data.
A catalogue record for this book is available from the British Library.

*This book is dedicated to the memory of my great friends,
Bill Gosden (poet, philosopher and perpetual student)
and his wife, Kath, who both passed away during
the year in which this book was written.*

CONTENTS

ACKNOWLEDGEMENTS

I would like to thank my wife, Ann, for tolerating me spending hours in my den tapping with one finger on my laptop and laughing at my own jokes. Secondly, thanks to my son, Clive, for doing the "computer" bits which are beyond my comprehension and my daughter, Melanie, for her critical perusal of the book.

Also, I would like to thank Jeremy Thompson of The Book Guild and his production and marketing staff for guiding me through the publication process.

PREFACE

My wife and I love Stanwick Lakes in Northamptonshire and walk there early nearly every morning with our dog, Caillou. We walk various routes and always see new and different things, particularly as the seasons change. Also, we have made many friends on our walks and have met interesting and genial people.

Stanwick Lakes and the surrounding Nene valley countryside are an area of notable natural beauty. Stanwick Lakes is not only a Site of Special Scientific Interest (SSSI) but it is part of the Nene Valley Nature Improvement Area (NIA) which recognises it as one of England's top nature areas. Furthermore, its European designation is of a level of importance equal to areas such as the Camargue in France.

In addition to its natural beauty, Stanwick Lakes is a site with a fascinating history. Before gravel extraction began, archaeological investigation revealed thousands of years of human occupation of the site. Neolithic (c 3700 – 3500 BC) long barrows (burial mounds) were found as well as Bronze Age (c 2500 – 1500 BC) round barrows.

Evidence of Iron Age (c 400 BC – 43 AD) occupation was found in the remains of around fifty roundhouses then, near that site, the remains of a Roman villa (c 250 – 400 AD) were revealed.

Towards the north end of the lakes evidence of a Saxon (c 950 AD) water mill and timber hall were discovered; a later Norman manor house was also found to have been built on the same site surrounded by a hamlet called West Cotton which continued to be occupied until the mid-fifteenth century.

Therefore, all this natural beauty and very interesting history make Stanwick Lakes an ideal location for country walks.

***

As well as being good exercise, walking in the countryside has a spiritual and therapeutic dimension. I believe most country-lovers find they have a primeval urge to forsake synthetic civilisation and return home to the natural environment in which they originated and are most contented. This escapist sentiment is expressed beautifully in my favourite poem, *Goodbye,* by Ralph Waldo Emerson.

> *Goodbye proud world! I'm going home.*
> *Thou art not my friend, and I'm not thine.*
> *Long through thy weary crowds I roam,*
> *A river-ark on the ocean brine,*
> *Long I've been tossed like the driven foam;*
> *But now, proud world! I'm going home.*

Goodbye to flattery's fawning face;
To Grandeur with his wise grimace;
To upstart Wealth's averted eye;
To supple Office, low and high;
To crowded halls, to court and street;
To frozen hearts and hasting feet;
To those who go and those who come;
Goodbye, proud world! I'm going home.

I'm going to my own hearth-stone,
Bosomed in yon green hills alone –
A secret nook in a pleasant land
Whose groves the frolic fairies planned;
Where arches green, the livelong day
Echo the blackbird's roundelay
And vulgar feet have never trod,
A spot that is sacred to thought and God.

O, when I am safe in my sylvan home,
I tread on the pride of Greece and Rome;
And when I am stretched beneath the pines,
Where the evening star so holy shines,
I laugh at the lore and pride of man,
At the sophist schools and the learned clan;
For what are they all in their high conceit,
When man in the bush with God may meet.

This book is the story (often flippant) of the year, 2016, on my walks round the lakes with my wife, Ann, the things we see, the thoughts we have and the pleasure we experience. However, I do not profess to be an expert naturalist but merely someone who has gathered information through a lifetime of walking in the countryside and being interested in the things around me. Therefore, I apologise if those with greater knowledge find I have misidentified anything or made incorrect observations.

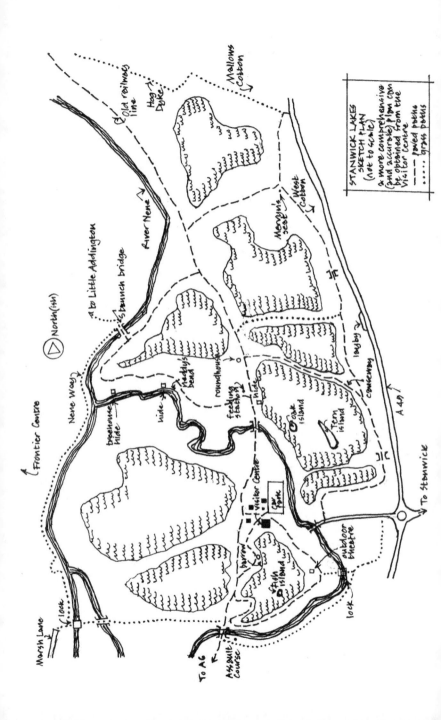

JANUARY

1 January. 8.15am. I wake up; I open my eyes – well, one of them, the other one's stuck – gunked up; I nudge it open with my knuckle. I haven't slept well, my body being hot-wired by excessive alcohol at a New Year's Eve party. I need more sleep and turn over hoping that Morpheus, God of Sleep, will accept me back in his arms a bit longer. Before shutting my eyes, I look down the bed; Caillou, our Westie is standing in the bedroom doorway looking pleadingly at me; he is already thirty minutes late for his morning walk; he wants to go – no, he needs to go – no, he MUST go.

I nudge Ann awake; we give up hope of more sleep and get up.

After a sobering coldish shower and a quick breakfast, we load Caillou into the car and head off for our first morning walk of the year at Stanwick Lakes. Except this year it will be different; I have made a resolution, a promise to myself that during 2016, when I return home I will write about the things we see, the facts we learn, the people we meet and the thoughts I have (bonkers though they may sometimes be).

So off I go to start my new role as a Literary Dog Walker.

***

The temperature is 1C when we arrive at the lakes. There has been an overnight frost (one of the few we have had this winter) but the white ground cover is rapidly thawing.

It seems spring just can't wait to arrive; leaf buds are already on some hawthorns and even the first signs of their flowers. Also, the post-Christmas catkins are on the hazel trees dangling like yellowy-green fashionable earrings.

Around this time of year, we start looking for the first wildflowers but already there are flowers on some white dead-nettles, and, in places, the ever-present daisies dot the grass. I hope the weather does not worsen and nature regrets its haste.

The day is windless and the waters merely mirrors as I watch a solitary pair of shelducks on a lake past the roundhouse. At the feeding station, some mallards and hen pheasants forage on the ground while blue tits and great tits raid the hanging feeders; a dunnock creeps through the bushes nearby. Great tits have a varied repertoire of calls but today we are surprised to hear, what we call, their "squeaky bike pump" song which we usually expect later in the spring.

The windless weather is a contrast to recent days when storm Frank has brought more misery to already blighted areas of the north and west of the UK. Strange how the weather has got much worse since we started naming storms.

I still have a boozy headache so I have decided it's not worth feeling so grotty and have made a resolution to give up alcohol for this year.

***

I read in the *Evening Telegraph* yesterday about some proposed developments near Stanwick Lakes. There are plans for an Asda store at Warth Park, Raunds near the north end of the lakes and, at the south end, a developer wishes to demolish the football stadium and build a retail park; there are already plans for an Aldi store on land adjacent to the stadium. All this is in addition to the retail park currently being constructed at Rushden lakes. While, to a certain extent I welcome these new developments because they bring facilities and employment to the area, I think we should take full advantage of the amenities of Stanwick Lakes before the Visitor Centre becomes a supermarket!

***

In the UK, last December was the second wettest ever but there has been a complete lack of frost and the average temperature was a record-breaking eight degrees centigrade, four degrees above average; what's going on? Global warming as well as global wetting! Apparently, it's because warmer air holds more moisture increasing the potential for heavy rainfall and flooding. This seems a poor excuse because, in my experience, the warmest European countries are the driest and the coldest ones the wettest.

But we are very lucky in this area and don't suffer from such heavy rainfall as other parts of the UK. As

I keep a fairly detailed diary, I decided to do some research. My wife and I walked at Stanwick Lakes on 296 occasions last year and it only rained on 23 (less than 8%) of our walks. Further research revealed that Northamptonshire is one of the driest parts of the country and is also one of the warmest having held the highest temperature record for nearly eighty years (source – Pitsford Hall weather station) – welcome to Costa del Stanwick!

While doing my weather research, I Googled "driest place in the UK" and found a website where people had submitted their views regarding the driest location. My favourite was that of one young wag who had written "my grandpa's drinks cabinet".

***

On the second of January, after heavy rain, the river was in spate and the water levels at their highest for some months. On our walk, I stopped at the river bridge; detritus washed downstream had snagged on the overhanging branches of a willow and collected there forming a "mini-dam". I hoped the water levels would soon drop and the debris be released to continue its journey towards the North Sea. However, two days later, after more rain, the "mini-dam" became a "maxi-dam" partially blocking the river and sending the main flow over the bank to flood nearby meadows. The path alongside the river was also inundated causing us to divert our walk.

I shall have to stop bleating on about this being the driest part of the country because, the following day, heavy rain had flooded more of the paths. The rangers had closed the paths around the river and past Mervyn's seat, so today, the fifth, we did the Layby Walk but still had to paddle through a stretch of the main path between the bird hide and the roundhouse. I checked my diary and found that the last time we were unable to walk round the river because of floods was the thirty-first of May 2014, nineteen months ago.

***

The wide main path through the centre of the lakes is the route of the old Northampton to Peterborough railway which was axed in 1963 by Dr Beeching. The line was built in 1843, the engineer being Robert Stephenson. To avoid flooding it was built mainly on an embankment and was a single track with passing sections. Today, as well as conveniently providing a level path for walkers, it is also a designated traffic-free cycle route. Often, while walking along the path, it is noticeable that the river or lake water level on one side of the embankment is several feet higher than on the other side; so, without the embankment the whole area would be one vast flood plain – and Stanwick Lakes as we know it couldn't exist. At least we've got something to thank Beeching for!

***

We see munjac regularly at the moment, probably because their usual stamping grounds are rain-sodden; about the size of a Labrador dog, the munjac is the runt of the deer family. There was a munjac grazing on an area of grass near the river and as we approached, it raised its head to stare at us. As we got nearer it nonchalantly sauntered into the thicket giving us one last cursory glance as if to say, 'it's only them!'

The shy munjac deer is also called the barking deer because of the doglike bark it makes when threatened or distressed. It is one of the oldest deer, remains having been dated to before prehistoric times. They were introduced to Britain around the beginning of the twentieth century and, after escaping from the Woburn estate in the 1970s, have spread throughout the UK. This rapid expansion is also attributable to their sexual habits: the does can breed at seven months old (not all that shy then!); they can conceive again within days of giving birth; they breed all year round with no rutting season like other deer and they live to between sixteen and nineteen years. All rather exhausting, isn't it? No wonder they spend most of their time lying around in thickets and are only active at dawn and dusk.

8 January. My no-alcohol resolution is still holding although, for medicinal reasons, I have been having a snifter of whisky because I heard it is good for keeping away coughs and colds.

Most of the small islands in the lakes have disappeared under an inch or two of water, their positions marked by puzzled gulls standing ankle deep in the water; they look around as if searching for the land which was here a few days ago.

Many of the familiar gulls (common, black-headed, herring and black-backed) are regular residents at the lakes. Some months ago, I met a birdwatcher, Steve, and asked him if he had seen anything interesting; he told me there was a glaucous gull about and where he had seen it, so the next day I went to that location. There were hundreds of all types of gull on a mudflat; I scanned across them with my binoculars but couldn't pick out anything extraordinary so all I can claim is that I have probably seen a glaucous gull, but which one of the hundreds it was I will never know.

Here's some information to help you identify a glaucous gull if you are lucky enough to encounter one. It is about the same size as a herring gull (i.e. one of the biggest ones) but doesn't have any black on its tail or wing tips; also, it is generally paler in colour. Best of luck, but it will take me some practice to identify one with certainty.

Glaucous gulls are winter visitors from the Arctic with the largest numbers appearing in Scotland. In England, they are mostly coastal but, being scavengers, they often join other gulls to raid rubbish dumps etc., so you probably wouldn't want to associate with them anyway.

***

In the small lake near the Visitor Centre there is an island on which there is a wooden sculpture of a fish; it currently has a large hole in the middle where there was once a round basketwork body. Unfortunately, this basketry disintegrated during a storm and was blown away. Hopefully, one day the person who sculptured the fish will row to the island and perform some restorative surgery on it.

Last summer, after a long dry spell, the fish sculpture disappeared in the thriving island vegetation, but now that has gone, it stands silhouetted lonely against the lake water.

**

On our walks recently, we have noticed small tufts of greyish fur by the paths. These tufts are the results of buck rabbits fighting. At this time of the year, as the mating season is about to begin, they fight for dominance in their group and for the best nesting sites. Rabbits only live for about a year but are very active during that time. The does can produce more than twenty young a year and begin breeding when only a few months old; also, the bucks mate with several does. Their gestation period is about a month so, at this production rate, we should be wading around in bunnies but we get a three-month respite as they cease breeding between October and January. Also we can thank foxes, badgers, weasels, minks and other predators for keeping the numbers down.

Rabbits are very territorial and rarely stray more than two hundred yards from their burrow; the bucks mark the boundary with droppings and scent from their glands. When a rabbit spots danger, it usually freezes then warns others by thumping its hind feet on the ground. Their white tails are conspicuous but act as a warning sign to other rabbits as they run for cover.

In folklore rabbits are often portrayed as tricksters capable of cunningly outwitting their enemies. This skill caused them to be considered a symbol of good luck and consequently people carried a rabbit's foot to protect them; there is evidence of this practice as far back as 600 BC. Rabbits were also called "moon rabbits" because certain shapes on the moon could be interpreted as representing a rabbit.

While I am rabbiting on (from Cockney rhyming slang for "rabbit and pork" meaning "talk") I will relate an incident from my childhood. When I was about four years old it was common for people to keep rabbits which ended up on the dinner table. We had a hutch in our garden, and when we had some baby rabbits, one of them only had one eye; my father nicknamed it Nelson and it became my favourite. Some months later as I sat at the table my mother brought in a casserole and I asked what we were having for dinner; my elder brother heartlessly told me it was Nelson. I sobbed for ages and didn't eat a thing but full bellies were more important than sentiment in those days. This incident has always remained vivid in my memory and left me with an affectionate attachment to rabbits.

**

As we stand chatting to our friend, Jane, with her dog, Barney, there are huge dense flocks of lapwings roiling across the sky in a synchronised flickering avian ballet. They all sway and change direction together as though controlled by a divine choreographer. When they turn upwards showing their white undersides they almost become invisible against the sky then, at the flick of a swirl, they reappear as hundreds of black specks. The cloud of birds drops down to a lake island but at the very last moment aborts the landing and spirals upwards again. Spectacular! Is there a purpose to all this or do they do it just for fun? Apparently, these are male lapwings performing display flights over their breeding territories – so just blokes showing off really.

***

Nearly every morning at this time of year, there is a grey heron at exactly the same spot which is on a strip of land next to a narrow channel between two lakes. This is the heron's angling pitch and I often wondered why he is always attracted to that particular place. The answer is that the brook flowing down from Stanwick village enters the small nearer lake raising its water level; the water then flows through the gap into the other lake and fishes are carried in this current past the heron and, bingo! – Mr. Heron gets a takeaway.

14 January. So far, apart from my daily snifter, I have abstained from alcohol but I am bothered about what I am going to do with the bottles of fine wine I have been given as Christmas presents; probably the odd glass with my dinner at weekends needn't be considered a breach of my resolution.

At 7.45 a.m. as we arrive at the lakes the temperature is one degree; it is dark, it is raining, there is a scything south westerly and it's about as miserable as the weather can be, so we just walk round the small lake near the Visitor Centre. Also, these conditions are not binoculars or camera friendly so I mope along in the gloom scowling at the few coots barmy enough to surf the waves.

***

Next to the main path (old railway line) is a piece of sculpture, but don't think Venus de Milo. This erection of four, twelve-metre-high vertical columns with numerous cross pieces somewhat resembles scaffolding, but to appreciate its beauty (?) it is necessary to know its *raison d'être*. This sculpture is part of the Changing Track project which celebrates the existence of former railways and there are similarly inspired installations in County Mayo, Ireland and Catalonia in Spain. The artist who created the work was Catalonian, Xevi Bayona, and it was funded by Northamptonshire County Council and the European Union (which may have some influence on the way I vote in the forthcoming referendum on whether to stay in or leave).

16 January: heavy frost: minus two degrees. The furry buds of the pussy willows that were beginning to appear seem to have retreated into their husks. I know how they feel; I struggled to prise myself from under the warmth of the duvet this morning and got up about forty-five minutes later than usual. On this day in 1945 Adolf Hitler retreated into his Fuhrerbunker under the garden of the Reich Chancellery in Berlin; somebody else who couldn't stand the cold.

***

The Mystery of the Missing Maxi-dam: The river dam of debris, which beavers would have been proud of, has disappeared. I stood on the bridge and looked puzzled downstream; the previously diverted river was flowing unimpeded on its normal course without the huge build-up of detritus under the willow tree. How could this have happened? The river water level hadn't dropped low enough for the flotsam to float away under the willow boughs. I wandered on trying to think what force of nature had intervened. Could a strong surge of water from upstream have had enough power to push away the dam of branches, twigs and rubbish that had been getting bigger every day? Could the weight of the build-up have snapped the overhanging branches thereby releasing the debris? No explanation I could think of seemed plausible so I remained mystified.

Then, a couple of days later, I mentioned the conundrum to Luke, the head ranger, and he solved it immediately. Two of the rangers had been to the riverbank with a pole saw and other long reaching equipment and hacked, sawn, poked and prodded at the dam until it had broken up and floated off downstream. Bravo! It must have been a difficult and even slightly risky job to lean over the swirling torrent to do that – fiendishly resourceful, our rangers.

***

Here be dragons:

Our friend, Christiana, who walks with her Scottie, Margo, seems talented at spotting wildlife, particularly mammals, that we don't see; probably because she often also walks at dusk. Today when we meet her she is in a state of extreme excitement.

'Guess what I've seen,' she says.

'What was it?' I ask.

'It was enormous; I was quite scared.'

'What sort of creature?'

'I was with Jane but she didn't see it because she had her back to it.'

I start to search my memory for any recent reports of zoo escapees.

'Was it big?' I ask.

'It walked across the path only about twenty yards away. It was quite frightening.'

At this point I resolve never to walk at the lakes again unless escorted by an armed Bantu askari.

'It seemed black and was about this big.' Christiana shows me fisherman-like with her hands that it was around two feet long. 'I think it was a mink.'

A sense of relief but also disappointment seeps over

me and I am puzzled because I know mink are only ferret-sized.

The sighting was reported to, and discussed with, the rangers and, because of its size, the majority verdict was that it was an otter. They are not uncommon along the river but are rarely seen.

At around the same time, I was chatting with the head ranger, when Rossi with her dog Shadow came and reported that she had seen a big, mainly brown, animal which she said may have had some white on it. 'A munjac,' we suggested. 'No, bigger than that, bigger than a dog!' This time we concluded it was probably a roe deer; they occasionally pass through the lakes area but so far have not taken up residency.

22 January. I went to a meeting at the local pub last night and, before I could get to the bar to order a fruit juice, a pal of mine had brought me a pint of my favourite beer; it tasted wonderful but it must be considered an isolated breach of my no alcohol rules.

The temperature early in the week was minus five degrees and it was frosty; today it has risen to five degrees but there is a price to pay – it is raining!

The rise in temperature has triggered procreation urges in the coots. In the water, they rise on their tails in pairs then square up to one another before noisily pattering off trying to mount each other's backs. I am not sure whether this is the first attempts at mating or males chasing off rivals. I feel like telling them to take it easy, there will be plenty of time for that later.

Coots can be vicious towards each other and have fierce fights over territory particularly during the mating season which starts in mid-March. Also, unlike ducks, after diving they bring their catch to the surface which leads to more fights and squabbling. The white patch on their foreheads has given rise to the expression "bald as a coot" (for some reason, always a bit hurtful to me when I hear it).

A heron soars overhead and then the huge bird banks away to make a slow, steady approach to the edge of the lake before lowering its legs like an undercarriage for a careful controlled landing: doors to manual: thank you for flying with Heron Airlines.

24 January. There was a RSPB Garden Bird watch event at the lakes today. Bob Webster, the local bird expert, was leading bird watching walks and a group of enthusiasts was catching birds in fine nets, ringing them then releasing them. We have participated in bird ringing sessions in the past and would recommend them. It is wonderful to have an almost weightless, recently born, blue tit chick in the palm of your hand.

Today I overheard some of the bird enthusiasts debating whether a bird they had seen was a Siberian chaffinch. It had been netted and they had been able to handle it but were still uncertain what it was. Such discussions make me feel ornithologically inadequate. 1. I have never heard of a Siberian chaffinch. 2. What's Stanwick got that Siberia hasn't?

***

Near the back of the Visitor Centre is a rather unimpressive mound of earth surrounded by a fence. This is actually an ancient monument, a Bronze Age barrow dating to between 2500 – 1500 BC. This barrow is believed to be part of a network of similar burial sites in the area which were in use for over 1500 years. During archaeological investigations skeletal remains of a man, believed to be a chieftain, were discovered.

I have noticed on my visits to the lakes that there are a lot of men called Dave about; one of the rangers is called Dave and several chaps we meet on our walks are Daves; here Daves outnumber all other male Christian names. On that basis, I think there is a strong possibility that the Bronze Age chieftain buried beneath the barrow could have been called Dave.

It is amazing to imagine prehistoric Dave and his pals wandering around in the Stanwick Lakes area about 4000 years ago, long before the parking charges were introduced.

Dave was buried with his possessions, and pottery and flint daggers as well as bone tools were found. Some of Dave's chattels are displayed at the Visitor Centre.

Today the barrow has become a burrow as it is the favourite hangout of rabbits which are possibly attracted to the voids beneath the ground.

Also discovered in the barrow was the skull of an auroch, a huge prehistoric wild ox. This was an ancestor of domestic cattle but was much larger, the height of the bulls averaging 1.8 metres [6 feet] to the shoulders. They resembled Spanish fighting bulls and there is a depiction of one on the Heritage Trail stone next to the barrow. Scientific analysis of the teeth suggests that the animal was not local but had come from a region of older rocks (e.g. Peak District, Malvern Hills); it was probably brought here to be part of a burial ceremony and later slaughtered.

The thought of these beasts trundling about in the fields outside Irthlingborough is quite disconcerting but we need not be concerned because the last one died in Poland in 1627; the poor creatures had been hunted to extinction. However, they had a long earthly existence as the oldest remains of them, found in India, dated back two million years. It is believed they migrated to Europe around 270,000 years ago which makes the presence of human life on this planet very insignificant. I wonder if our race will be around in two million years!

28 January. The storm that has dumped record depths of snow on the eastern seaboard of the United States has tracked across the Atlantic and its tail is now battering us. Fortunately, the storm mellowed en route; the tail is wagging less vigorously here and, instead of bringing snow, we are merely being lashed by high winds.

There is a definite strategy for having a tolerable walk at the lakes in such conditions. The tactic is to leave the car park at the end opposite the Visitor Centre with the wind at your back, and then, and this is the worst part, turn right at the roundhouse across the causeway; here it is very exposed and you receive a strapping salvo from the right. Hang onto your hats until you reach the shelter of the wood; then you can return unbuffeted back to the car park.

The storm now blasting us is called Gertrude; they have only just starting naming storms in alphabetical order and we are up to "G" already. Gertrude is from the German for "spear of strength" (*ger* – spear, *thrud* – strength) which accounts for the sharpness of the wind. The most famous Gertrude is Hamlet's incestuous mother, the Queen of Denmark; I knew there was something perverse about this storm when it first arrived.

***

On reflection, because I now have a daily snifter and a glass or two of wine with my meals plus the occasional pint of beer, I suppose that, theoretically, I have broken my vows of abstinence. Well, I started out with good intentions but it seems circumstances conspired against me or my body wasn't ready to enter the dark uncertain world of temperance. I'll maybe try again next year.

FEBRUARY

1 February. The mute swans are beginning to claim their breeding territories in lakes and along stretches of river; they assemble in pairs, or occasionally with last autumn's cygnets, and fiercely defend their patch. A pair or family will not tolerate another swan arriving on their chosen domain. If an intruder lands, war ensues and we have often stood and watched these skirmishes. An adult swan, presumably a male, maximises its size by lifting its prow, hunching its shoulders, semi-spreading its wings and arcing its neck like a cobra about to strike. It then sails at a top rate of knots at its adversary, launching pecking blows on its back if it gets close enough. It is a persistent and relentless attack and the assailant will not stop until the interloper gives up and flies off. The swan then resumes its normal posture and swims back to its partner presumably with smug self-satisfaction at a battle well fought and won.

In Greek mythology, the god Zeus took the form of a swan and seduced and raped Leda, the wife of Tyndareos, the king of Sparta. So perhaps the swan we watched was not chasing off an intruder but was practising for a more sinister activity later.

They are called mute swans because it was once

believed that they did not make a sound but anyone who has had to negotiate round a swan blocking their path knows they can make some very aggressive snorts and hisses. It was also believed that swans only sang before dying which gave rise to the word "swansong" – a final performance or activity before retiring.

Furthermore, it was erroneously thought that swans mated for life and they therefore became a symbol of fidelity, but they are now known to sometimes "divorce" and take new partners – typical of modern times!

2 February. Today is Candlemas Day which Christians celebrate as the purification of Mary forty days after the birth of Jesus and the day when he, in accordance with Jewish tradition, was taken to the temple to be presented to God. Candlemas gets its name from the old custom of taking candles into church on this day to be used throughout the year; they were blessed during a Mass – hence Candlemas.

It is also the midpoint of winter being halfway between the shortest day and the spring equinox in March when the sun is directly over the equator and the length of night and day is equal.

So, what has Candlemas got to do with our walk today at Stanwick Lakes? Well it was believed that the weather on Candlemas Day determined the weather for the rest of the winter; if it is fine and bright then there is more winter to come, if it is cloudy, wet and stormy winter's weather is almost over. An old proverb echoes this:

If Candlemas Day be fair and bright,
Winter will have another fight.
If Candlemas Day brings cloud and rain,
Winter won't come again.

When we started our walk this morning it was cloudy and windy, and it began to spit with rain as we finished. Good news, I thought, no more winter weather. But by nine o'clock the sky had cleared and it was sunny for the rest of the day so if the pundits of old are right there is still more winter to come.

***

Who trusted God was love indeed,
And love Creation's final law –
Tho' nature, red in tooth and claw,
With ravine, shreik'd against his creed.

Although this verse from Alfred Tennyson's *In Memoriam* refers to humanity, I am often reminded of the third line on my walks. Recently we found the bloody, headless body of a hen pheasant by the side of the path and on two previous occasions we had discovered similarly butchered corpses of swans. They had all been killed by foxes. The assassins had left a bloody mess by biting into the birds and gorging on their innards but had left the rest intact apart from beheading them. I do not know what use the foxes find for such mementoes, presumably they take them back to their dens, have them mounted and hung on the walls like stag hunting souvenirs in a Scottish laird's castle.

We report these findings to the rangers who remove the gory carcasses so as not to upset sensitive walkers and visitors who might be distressed at encountering them.

***

There is evidence of other poetry lovers visiting the lakes. A new seat has been sited towards Mervyn's bench and the inscription on it, dedicated to Connie and Susan, is from *The Windhover* by Gerard Manley Hopkins.

> *No wonder of it: Sheer plod makes plough down sillion*
> *Shine, and blue-bleak embers, oh my dear,*
> *Fall, gall themselves, and gash gold-vermilion.*

A windhover is an old name for a kestrel and the poem has interpretations that connect it to bird watching. However, the poem is very allegorical and there have been many attempts to explain its meaning. The phrase on the seat refers to the fact that when a plough turns the earth, the sods [sillions] often shine due to the blade's action.

I will not intrude further into the donor's poetical motives for dedicating the seat except to state that I find the inscription beautiful, thought-provoking and moving. Thank you, whoever you are!

I, too, am often inspired to express my most profound thoughts poetically; here is a recent effort.

There once was a young lass from Stanwick,
Whose short skirts caused quite a panic,
The hem was so high,
It revealed most of her thigh,
And made the local lads manic.

OK, so maybe it's not great poetry but even Shakespeare wrote some saucy verses. For the information of non-locals "Stanwick" is pronounced without the "w".

8 February. After last week's storm Henry, Imogen has arrived today. At the rate we are getting through the alphabet, we will be having storm Zacharias by the end of March and, as each storm seems to be stronger than its predecessor, this one could be of biblical magnitude; start building the ark!

On the subject of arks, I believe there are some creatures Noah should never have bothered to save; I am thinking particularly of mosquitoes and mink. If I had been around in Noah's time I would have crept into his cabin, found his clipboard and erased those two from his salvation list.

Anyone who has been on a Mediterranean holiday knows it can be blighted by red itchy sores caused by mosquitoes feeding on their bodies. However, minks can be a similar blight on the world of small fauna and seem to have no useful purpose other than, as coats, adorning the curvaceous bodies of starlets from the 1950s.

I have seen minks a couple of times at the lakes and their favourite hunting grounds are the lake fringes where they feast on the eggs and young of ground nesting birds. The rangers attempt to prevent this by setting traps to catch the mink and I regularly check the traps to see if they have been sprung. So far they have only had occasional success but they have trapped around sixteen in the last eighteen months. Dave, the ranger, showed me one that had been captured; it was in a cage in the ranger's shed; it hissed and spat at is. They are vicious and fearless creatures that will even attack a dog if cornered.

Mink are of the same family as otters, and were introduced from America to be farmed to produce pelts to make mink coats. Escapees have spread throughout the British Isles and, being good swimmers, they also feed on fish as well as small mammals. Although the guidebooks illustrate them as shiny dark brown, the ones I have seen seemed jet black. Also, a couple of times when crossing the causeway bridges, I have heard them, underneath the bridge, hiss at our dog but by the time I have looked for them they have scampered away in a rustling of reeds. As they have no natural predators, their numbers are increasing rapidly in the UK to the detriment of many indigenous species.

10 February. Ash Wednesday, the first day of Lent, a time of fasting and resolutions: I will be giving up Brussel sprouts again this year! Although it is still cold and windy, the small birds are becoming noisier and chirpier at the prospect of spring, their activity being triggered by longer daylight hours.

As we walk along, a band of goldfinches, one of our most colourful and pretty birds, bobs over the tops of thistles in front of us; they have a few pecks then flit to the next patch of thorny peaks. This bird's attachment to thistles is endorsed by their French name, *chardonneret*, which is derived from *chardon,* the French for thistle. Also, in this country in Anglo Saxon times they were known as "thisteltuiges" or "thistletweakers" but their current name is from the old English, "goldfinc" which they acquired due to the golden yellow stripe on their wings seen when they are flying. Their collective name is actually a "charm" from the Latin meaning a magical song or spell.

John Keats accurately conveyed the beauty, colour and actions of goldfinches in his poem, *I stood tip-toe upon a Little Hill.*

Sometimes goldfinches one by one will drop
From low hung branches; little space they stop;
But sip, and twitter, and their feathers sleek;
Then off at once, as in a wanton freak:
Or perhaps, to show their black and golden wings,
Pausing upon their yellow fluttering.
Were I in such a place. I surely should pray,
That nought less sweet, might call my thoughts away.

14 February. Appropriately for Saint Valentine's Day, in the woods clusters of the large arrowhead-shaped viridian green leaves of Lords and Ladies are pushing through. This plant is the porn star of the wildflower world because parts of it were considered to resemble human genitalia; in those days, they had a vivid imagination unsullied by too much television. The cowl-like green sheave (spathe) resembles a vagina and the brownish purple stem (spadix) a penis. Also, because of this sexual suggestiveness, the plant was believed to be a powerful aphrodisiac but the berries of the plant are poisonous causing severe irritation of the mouth, tongue and stomach. This has resulted in many attendances at hospital A&E departments for accidental plant poisoning.

Its botanical name *arum maculatum* derives from *aron,* the Greek for "poisonous plant" and *maculatus,* Latin for "speckled", because the leaves are spotted.

This plant has over a hundred names among them: cuckoo pint (rhymes with "mint"): stallions and mares: dog's dibble: wake-robin: Adam and Eve: Jack in the pulpit: fairy lamps (because the plant's pollen glows at night).

However, it was the prim Victorians who promulgated the name Lords and Ladies to rid the plant of its embarrassing sexual connotations.

Botany can never be a boring study when such salacious facts can be discovered!

I will resist the temptation to include some poetry about Lords and Ladies because the only appropriate piece I know is from a song I learnt during my rugby playing days. I will also refrain from writing about great tits for the time being.

***

I stand watching about five male and female blackbirds foraging on the ground in the wood and they seem to be operating to a prescribed work pattern.
1. Spread out about ten metres apart.
2. Take turns to remain stock-still.
3. Cock head to one side and listen.
4. Hop across the ground a few metres.
5. Take a few savage pecks at ground.
6. Toss leaves away with sideways flick of head.
7. Stab at something on ground.
8. Eat snack.
9. Repeat entire sequence.
10. If disturbed, fly into branches above and remain there listening with the occasional statutory cock of the head.
11. Return to ground when threat passes.
12. Carry on doing this all day until fed up, full up or tired.

Also, amongst the bird-gang is a redwing but it has a different agenda; it is interested in whatever might be beneath some logs and pecks away for an alternative menu choice.

20 February. A noisy skein of about twenty Canada geese flies overhead; all at the same time they are loudly honking advice and opinions to each other like MPs at Prime Minister's Question Time. Their call has been likened to the baying of hounds. However, at this time of year, the flocks are beginning to break up as they split into pairs, their thoughts on matters other than communal living. The paired-up geese stand very close to each other whilst feeding on grass and reeds, then they pause and canoodle by rubbing necks. All this is very cute but later in the year, when they have had their goslings, they will become a nuisance by wandering around in flocks on the paths and grassy areas depositing their piles of slimy green droppings for us to step in. They are largely predisposed to ignore people so at our approach they casually waddle off into the water.

Large populations of Canada geese can cause problems in the lakes as they often defecate in the water. These nutrient-high droppings encourage algae and plant growth leading to algae blooms and excessive water vegetation in the summer.

23 February. On Tern Island, the gulls are making a raucous racket, flapping about on the ground, flying up, wheeling around then dropping back down again all whilst screeching and squawking as loud as they can. A flock of black-headed gulls, already shrieking excitedly, is winging over to join them. Amongst the gulls on the ground, some lapwings squat ignoring the hullabaloo around them and stubbornly refusing to surrender their already-claimed nesting sites to the noisy gulls. I am afraid we are going to have to tolerate this racket for some time and it will get much worse in a couple of months when the terns arrive.

***

A party of small birds flits along the willow wands and at first, as I merely glimpse a blackish head, I think they are goldfinches, but when I train my binoculars on them I see they are reed buntings. Although the males have a black head, it is divided by a white line from the corners of the beak so the black lower part looks like a drooping gaucho-style moustache. We are fortunate to have so many reed buntings here because their numbers have seriously declined since the 1970s. Our attention is often drawn to them by their tinkling repetitive song as they perch conspicuously on the tops of reeds then they drop down onto the ground where they creep about for food.

***

A grey squirrel tight-ropes rapidly along a branch then acrobatically scales a vertical trunk. It is the first one I have seen for some time and although, contrary to common belief, they do not hibernate, they sensibly remain in their dreys when it is particularly cold.

Grey squirrels are another species introduced into the UK by the Victorians and they were released in over thirty sites between 1876 and 1930. Since then their numbers have increased while those of the native red squirrel have seriously declined. It is estimated that there are about two million grey squirrels now, compared with 160,000 red squirrels which have retreated into ever more remote areas.

Incidentally, the male squirrels are called "bucks", the females "does" and the young "kittens".

I sometimes wonder what our ancestors thought they were going to achieve by these introductions of foreign species. As well as grey squirrels, we now have munjacs and minks all over the UK which are all multiplying at an expeditious rate. I think we should be thankful that the Victorians did not believe that crocodiles would be useful here.

24 February. I am trying not to get too excited but some wildflowers are starting to appear. A couple of days ago I saw a solitary speedwell, yesterday a few red dead-nettles and today several coltsfoot. By far the most interesting of these is the dandelion-like coltsfoot, the yellow flowers of which only open on sunny days. Coltsfoot has been used as an herbal medicine for thousands of years and its botanical name, *tussilago,* means "cough dispeller". I should say 'don't try this at home' but to make a cough cure the recipe is to put one or two teaspoons of the leaves or flowers (it is generally recommended to only use the leaves) in a cup of boiling water, leave it to cool and sip a small dose every two hours, drinking no more than three cups daily. Coltsfoot can also be dried and smoked like tobacco when it is considered to be an effective remedy for bronchitis and asthma. Lastly, it can be made into a poultice and used as a treatment for sores, burns, eczema and insect bites. I apologise if I have just put a few chemists out of business!

28 February. As it is less muddy, this morning for the first time for several months, we walk along the Nene Way footpath which is outside Stanwick Lakes reserve and is reached by a ramped steel bridge.

Today we met several fishermen and when we chatted to one of them he showed us a photograph on his mobile phone of a fifteen-pound pike he had caught there yesterday. He also told us he had seen a kingfisher further along the river so as I walked along I carefully checked the overhanging branches to see if I could spot one. About three times I became excited when I saw a flash of turquoise but all I could claim is that I absolutely certainly identified a blue, small scrap of plastic.

The ramped steel pedestrian bridge is called the Staunch and it was built in 2010 by the County Council to replace a previous structure also called the Staunch. There has been a river crossing at this point since the seventeenth century to provide a footpath link between the villages of Stanwick and Little Addington. In 1761 the river Nene between the Wash and Northampton became navigable for the transportation of coal from the north east of England. At the Staunch a wooden gate was built which could be lowered to raise the water level and facilitate the passing of boats over the shallows.

MARCH

1 March. The first day of meteorological spring: To quote Robin Williams, 'Spring is nature's way of saying, let's party!'

Grey herons versus little egrets: On one of the small lakes there are both birds standing in the reeds waiting for a passing fish but one thing puzzles me; the grey heron is well camouflaged in the reeds and is often difficult to spot, whereas the little egret has the same habitat but, having pure white plumage, stands out in the shrubbery. What is the difference in their fishing strategies that allows them both to be equally successful when their guise is strongly contrasted? This is my conclusion: when a little fish in the water looks up, the heron is concealed in the reeds; when it looks upwards at a little egret the bird, being white, is blended with the surrounding brightness of the sky.

Both of the birds are from the same family, *ardeidae,* but the little egret is about two thirds of the size of the heron which, with a six-foot wingspan, is our largest common land bird.

Another contrast is that the little egrets are mostly silent whereas grey herons make a loud croaking "kraark" call shortly after taking flight.

Little egrets easily launch themselves into the air but grey herons move skywards with slow ponderous wingbeats.

Little egrets were absent from the UK for centuries and only reappeared in the 1990s, breeding here for the first time at Brownsea Island in Dorset in 1996; however, in mediaeval times they were common in this country but became extinct due to hunting; they were a gourmet delicacy and, in 1465, a thousand egrets were on the menu at Cawood Castle to celebrate the enthronement of George Neville as the Archbishop of York. But equally, herons weren't escaping that fate as roast herons were also popular at mediaeval banquets.

The most unsettling fact about little egrets is that, because of their beautiful white feathers, in the nineteenth century they were hunted on the continent to provide plumes to decorate hats. In the first three months of 1887, one London dealer sold two million – I repeat – two million, egret skins. It's those bloody Victorians again!

So, which one wins the contest of the two *ardeidae*? – let's call it a draw!

3 March. A green woodpecker takes flight from the path in front of me, flies straight ahead with awkward hoppy wingbeats and then banks sideways into a wood. Later, twice I hear staccato drumming on a trunk and, as green woodpeckers rarely drum, I suspect this must be its cousin a great spotted woodpecker; anyway, some grubs or insects in a bark fissure have met their demise, unless the woodpecker's head-banging was the start of "foundation" work for a new residence.

***

I have started looking in at the bird feeding station more often now as the summer residents will soon start to arrive. Today, there is a cock pheasant strutting authoritatively about amongst a few mallard and moorhens while some great tits raid the hanging feeders above. As the leaves thicken on the surrounding trees the foliage will encroach further into the open space making the flight, for more timid birds, between concealment and food quicker and less perilous.

5 March. Oystercatcher Deficiency Syndrome: A few days ago, I received, by email, the Stanwick Lakes March newsletter and the first article I read stated that a pair of oystercatchers had been sighted at the lakes; I thought, *I go to the lakes every day and I haven't seen any; are oystercatchers avoiding me?* The next day I met a chap with some binoculars and whilst chatting to him he said he had just seen an oystercatcher. Again, I thought, *Why not me?* Today, just as I was nearing the car park and about to leave, I saw something black on the grass between the reeds on the far side of a small lake – *Something black, could be a mink!* So, I trained my binoculars on it and it was an oystercatcher. Suddenly, the world was alright with me.

Although oystercatchers are residents in this country they are not so common at Stanwick Lakes in the winter. Their name belies the food they prefer here and their presence is often revealed by scatterings of shells of freshwater mussels; they hammer these on the ground and prise them open with their orange-red bills.

6 *March*. There is a strong gusty wind and the sky is largely bereft of birds apart from a few crows that struggle to make headway. In their determination to reach their destination, they flap vigorously and are buffeted up and down like small plastic bin bags being blown overhead.

They are always rather noisy birds and those on the ground wander about with a waddle-strut. Even those on the tree tops maintain a croaking "kraa-kraa" commentary.

Crows are not colonial birds like their cousins, the rooks. There is an expression, 'If you see a rook on its own, it's a crow; if you see a flock of crows, they're rooks!'

There is a very interesting article about crows in the newspaper today. Researchers have found that crows have the same advanced thinking skills as chimpanzees, which they have developed over millions of years by facing the same challenges. The bird's cognition includes delaying gratification by hoarding food, using tools and thinking logically. During research, crows have dropped stones into a beaker to raise the liquid level so they can drink, and they are also able to recognise themselves in a mirror.

The scientists speculate that millions of years ago a common ancestor of apes and crows may have passed on a brain module they now both have.

I'll show more respect to crows in future!

9. March. Other members of the crow family, the magpies (scientific name *pica pica*) are forming large spring gatherings to resolve territorial disputes. I hear their "chacker chacker" calls in the woods and these will all be local magpies because they rarely stray from their birth places. These gatherings have two collective nouns, parliaments and ridings. They confidently strut or hop in their swanky black and white tuxedo plumage which, when it catches the light, has a bluish green sheen on the back and tail.

When I was young, children used to tell fortunes by the number of magpies they had seen together.

One for sorrow,
Two for joy,
Three for a girl,
Four for a boy,
Five for young,
Six for old,
Seven for a secret never to be told.

They were also nicknamed "admirals" and it was customary to salute when you saw them.

I was watching QI on television last night and Stephen Fry asked the two teams a Quite Interesting question. Where does the name "magpie" come from? After some trivial banter from Alan Davies et al, Stephen Fry informed them that the "pie" was from "pied," i.e. black and white, and the "mag" was an abbreviated form of "Margaret". In the middle ages, it was common for birds to be given Christian names, for example robin redbreast, jenny wren, tom tit and jack daw, but "mag" also meant "chatterer" which influenced the name chosen for magpies. Incidentally, the French for magpie is merely *pie* which confirms that the "mag" is an entirely English affix.

So whether you believe the "mag" is derived from "chatterer" or "Margaret" is up to you; take your *pica*!

10 March. Summary:
A month's rain in one day,
Foggy too, can't see much,
Nene valley on flood alert,
Meadows now one vast lake,
Most footpaths impassable,
Tern island under water,
Gulls bloody livid,
Burrows inundated,
Rabbits hopping mad,
Plant growth in stasis,
Reed nesting birds homeless,
Half marathon cancelled.
12 March.
At last some sun,
(England 25 Wales 21)

After that day of heavy rain, the water levels rose at the most rapid rate I, and the rangers, had known. From all paths being clear and dry one day, they were flooded in many places with water sweeping across them in torrents as one lake overflowed into another. The top fine gravel surface of the paths had been washed into the grass verges leaving potholes and depressions which the rangers will now need to arrange to reinstate. There is an old Northamptonshire word "warp" which describes the muddy and sandy deposit left on land after flooding; so that was what was covering the sides of the path.

I remember a similar situation some years ago; I met a local farmer at the lakes and he had come to move some cows, marooned in a corner of a flooded field, to a drier area. He had been warned in a phone call from the Environment Agency that more water was going to be released down the valley and that flood levels would rise rapidly. Within a short time, the field, where the cattle had been, was even more flooded.

The Environment Agency has a strategy for controlling the Nene valley water levels which is explained in their comprehensive document "The River Nene Catchment Flood Management Plan". Through this plan, when necessary, water is allowed to move down the Nene valley to empty the Northampton Washlands and Stanwick Lakes is considered a convenient place to allow water to accumulate as no housing or roadways are threatened. So, we are martyred for sacrificing our leisure amenity for the wellbeing of Northamptonians up the valley!

16 March. On the path by the railway bridge I find a sad sight, a freshly broken eggshell; this is the first evidence I have seen this year that egg-laying is in progress.

The egg is cream coloured and quite large, and has been stolen from a nest, smashed and the yoke eaten, probably by a mink or infanticide orientated bird. Fortunately, there is plenty of time for the egg-layer to start again.

Many birds start nesting in March and some as early as February. Chaffinches, great tits and blackbirds are some of the early starters. Blackbirds often have two or three broods during the summer, usually in March, May and July but sometimes as late as August. There are normally three to five eggs in each clutch and the chicks hatch in thirteen to fourteen days. They fledge about a fortnight later and learn to fly within the following week becoming independent of their parents in around three weeks. This is quite a rapid turnover but as many as 40% of them do not survive the egg and chick stage.

The nesting season for birds is defined in the Wildlife and Countryside Act 1981 as 1 March to 31 July. This is the reason hedge cutting, trimming and laying is carried out by farmers mainly in February as it is illegal to disturb the birds after 1 March if there are any signs of breeding activity.

***

Walking philosophy: Although the media news can be depressing, I find that when I am walking around the lakes, all these issues seem more remote as I become absorbed in looking around me at the wildlife. Then, as we head back home through the heavy traffic on the A45 and the Chowns Mill roundabout, the thoughts of the other troubled world seep back.

Walking is the most democratic of activities; most people can do it, it can be done almost anywhere and it requires no money but nowadays people do less walking than ever before in history.

Also, walking has long been known to have a mental benefit which was expressed in ancient Roman times by the Latin dictum *solvitur ambulando* which means "it is solved by walking".

This concept was first known in the fourth century when the Sophists suggested to Diogenes the Cynic in an argument that motion was unreal; Diogenes' counter-argument was simply to stand up and walk away – debate over, he solved it by walking. (Diogenes was also once seen begging for money from a statue and when asked why, he replied "I am practising disappointment").

Since then many prominent writers have conveyed the same concept in their works; Nietzche said that all great thoughts were conceived while walking and Hemingway would always walk along the quayside when he wanted to think things through. Henry David Thoreau stated that his thoughts began to flow as soon as his legs began to move and Bruce Chatwyn believed that walking was the best remedy to cure mental turmoil. More recently, the main character in Sebastian Faulks's novel *Where My Heart Used To Beat* expresses a similar sentiment when he says that all his life he has found that being in nature has helped him think.

So, if you feel overworked, burnt out, exhausted and

disconnected from the really important things, get your boots on and reconnect with creativity, wisdom and wellbeing.

19 March. I really need to brush up on my birdwatching skills. I can identify about sixty of the most common ones but my problems start in the spring when a lot of small, brownish summer visitors, mostly warblers, arrive then secrete themselves in the thickening foliage and tweet tauntingly at me. If I could pluck one from the bush or sky and turn it over in one hand while leafing through my bird guidebook in the other, my identification rate would vastly improve but unfortunately birds are not that obliging. I have studied one of these migrants through my binoculars and tied to memorise its salient characteristics but when I returned home and looked for it in my guidebook I found it could have been one of about a dozen.

My lack of experience in this respect was emphasised last night. We went to a dinner and were fortunate to chat to the guest of honour, countryside campaigner Kate Ashbrook, who had travelled some distance to the event so I asked her if she had a good journey. She told me she had arrived in the area earlier in the day spending the afternoon walking and birdwatching at Stanwick Lakes. I enthusiastically told her we walked there every morning and asked her if she had seen anything interesting. She said she had spent some time in a bird hide and seen dunlins, snipes and redshanks and heard a Cetti's warbler. Now, of these I have only seen redshanks a couple of times and wouldn't know a Cetti's warbler if I heard one. So, I felt a tinge of envy because an infrequent visitor had seen more in one visit than I do on my daily walks. So, more study, observation and patience required by me.

20 March. This morning, for a change, we walked at Kinewell (pronounced *kin–ee-well*) Lake at Ringstead. This lake is outside the boundary of the Stanwick Lakes Nature Reserve but is in the same chain of Nene Valley former gravel pits. It is one and a half miles around the lake so it is a leisurely three quarters of an hour's stroll. There is a small car park outside the village on the south west side. There are several advantages to walking at Kinewell Lake and one disadvantage. Firstly, dogs are allowed off their leads except for during the main nesting months of April, May and June; secondly, about halfway around the lake is the Woodford Mill tearoom, where one can stop for a drink or even lunch; thirdly, the lake is fringed by trees so even in the heat of summer (I wish) there is plenty of shade. The disadvantage is that not all the path around the lake is surfaced so it can be muddy during wet weather.

Kinewell Lake is the largest pocket park in Northamptonshire and is owned by Ringstead village. It is managed and maintained by volunteers of the Kinewell Lake Trust.

Today is warmer and brighter and a few more wildflowers are showing; there are some lesser celandines and ground ivies and, in the woods, a colourful display of daffodils and snowdrops presumably planted there by the village volunteers.

At Kinewell Lake some years ago I first saw Himalayan balsam; this is a pretty plant with Chinese lantern shaped pinkish flowers; however, this prettiness conceals its dark agenda as it is an introduced species which has become a major problem because it multiplies so quickly. It has now spread along the valley and has become abundant at Stanwick Lakes.

It was introduced into the UK in 1839 (those bloody Victorians again) as an ornamental garden plant. It grows to nearly three metres high and smothers other vegetation, and has spread due to its seed pods, which open explosively when ripe; they can shoot up to seven metres away and each plant can produce eight hundred seeds. So, admire it for its prettiness then curse it for its invasiveness.

21 March. Today is the second first day of spring. After the meteorological one on the first of March, it is the astronomical start of spring, so called because it is based on the earth's position relative to the sun in the northern hemisphere. Why do we need two first days of spring? Probably, because, in recent years, the nerdy weather bods have found it convenient to carve the year up into four equal chunks of three whole months.

Q. What's the difference between the first day of spring and the first spring day?

A. About a month.

The weather is not at all spring-like and storm Katie has swept across the Atlantic bringing stinging rain and strong winds. We did have a respite on Friday, the twenty-fifth, with an "out of the blue" day of clear skies and mild temperatures, and I believe I detected a slight increase in the greenish hue of some trees. Hawthorn and hazel are the front runners with the silver tips of the pussy willows a close third. Another sign of spring is the increasing absence of wigeon; they have been gathering in flocks in the riverside meadows, feeding heartily to build themselves up for their long migration northwards, and some have now departed for their summer dachas in Russia, Scandinavia and Iceland.

Male wigeon are easily identifiable by the creamy yellow stripe from their bill over their forehead, rather as though someone had flicked a blob of custard at them during a loutish dinner party.

Storm Katie was a bonus for departing wigeon; a few flaps up into its powerful south-westerly wind and they could hitch a ride north westward.

***

Stanwick Lakes is a brutal and savage place at the moment; Jane and Christiana (dogs: Barney and Margo) reported finding the bloodied corpse of a fox near the path last week which the rangers dispatched to the concealment of the bushes; Rossi and Helen (dogs: Shadow and Bobby) found, near the open-air theatre, a dead munjac with a gory wound on its neck; Doug, the cyclist, (no dog) told me he had seen a fox's head on his daily ride. Who's the culprit? There is the possibility that the fox and munjac could have limped into the Nature Reserve and died after a vehicle impact. However, foxes are known to be cannibalistic as the remains of other foxes have been found in their faeces and stomach content. They are opportunistic feeders and will eat whatever is available, which is the reason they are one of our most successful carnivores. Young foxes have even been known to eat their mothers, which makes the little darlings somewhat less endearing. Also, foxes are known to kill young munjac, but as the carcass found was quite large, I don't believe a fox was guilty on this occasion.

APRIL

April Fools' Day: The lady dog walkers at Stanwick Lakes are in a state of near swoon and flushed with high excitement today as I am wearing my shorts for the first time this year. However, unfortunately I suspect their excitement is due more to amusement than lust. My milky white pins are no longer the fine muscular specimens of my rugby playing days but thin knobbly sticks with a knee replacement scar down the middle. Of course, I tell the ladies it is a wound inflicted in battle. Also, worryingly when my dog notices my bare legs it stares at them and licks its lips.

Today is also the start of National Pets Month but we are trying to prevent our dog learning about this initiative as he gets spoilt enough anyway.

***

It is amazing what a magical effect the simple act of turning over the calendar seems to have on the great outdoors, that plus nature being encouraged by a few warmish days. On April the second, we walked round Marsh Lane leaving Stanwick Lakes at the A6 end, joining the Nene Way at the far side of the stadium then taking the lane before turning right at the lock to return to the Nature Reserve. It was not long before spring signs greeted us; over the river near the assault course the first sand martins of the year were swooping around. The smallest members of the swallow family they are the first ones to arrive from their winter homes in Africa and, unlike other migratory birds, they travel by day so they can feed on the wing.

We passed through clouds of midges which had awoken from their winter slumber to plague us. Later, in the green lane between the lock and the lakes, we found that some lady's smocks were in flower; these will adorn many damp grassy areas for a few months. They are also known as the "cuckoo flower" because their appearance often coincides with the arrival of the first cuckoo though I suspect we will have to wait some weeks before we hear one of those. Lady's smocks' pretty flowers range from white to pale lilac and there are many legends and folklores attached to them:

St. Helena found the smock of the Virgin Mary in a cave near Bethlehem; after, it was taken to St. Sophia then Aix la Chapelle where it was venerated, and the wildflower was named in honour of the relic.

It was believed that a thunderstorm would be caused if anyone picked the flower.

It was thought to generate lightning and shouldn't be taken into a house.

It was believed to attract adders and anyone who picked the flower would be bitten by one by the end of the year. (Actually, the plant is related to watercress and can be used in salads).

It is quoted by Shakespeare in *Loves Labours Lost*; 'lady smocks all silver white.'

Northamptonshire's most famous poet, John Clare, wrote of the flower in his poem, *The Wild-flower Nosegay*.

And wan-hued lady smocks, that love to spring
'side the swamp margin of some plashy pond;
And all in blooms that early Aprils bring,
With eager joy each fill'd my playful hand.

There is no record of John Clare causing a thunderstorm, being struck by lightning or being bitten by an adder but he probably quoted Shakespeare.

***

A concrete path at the end of a bridge near the lock is littered with fragments of mussel shells; this is a "crash site" used by birds, probably oystercatchers, to cleverly drop their mollusc gatherings to smash on the hard surface for an easy feast.

***

Recently the rangers and the volunteer group, the FOSiLs (Friends of Stanwick Lakes), have been restoring the Iron Age roundhouse and replacing the woven willow fence around it.

The replica Iron Age roundhouse was built close

to the site where an Iron Age settlement was found in 1985 during archaeological explorations before gravel quarrying began. The roundhouse was built between January and March 2011 as part of a community project involving over five hundred volunteers, schools and youth groups.

Lamentably, the thatched roof, which had taken four days to build, was destroyed by a fire started by vandals (wouldn't you just love to get your hands on them?) in March 2011; it was decided to replace the roof with a less flammable, but less authentic, alternative, and in October 2011 a turf roof was built.

In May 2011, to celebrate the completion of the replica, an event was held to demonstrate Iron Age crafts, and volunteers adorned the clothing of the time. I offered to come down in my loincloth but the rangers dissuaded me saying it could frighten off visitors.

There was evidence of about fifty timber framed Iron Age (400 BC – 43 AD) dwellings found at the site which shows that a significant farming community lived there growing bread-making grain and producing iron. They were also among the first peoples to use a coinage system and coins were also found at the site.

Coincidentally, an Iron Age settlement was also discovered at another Stanwick in North Yorkshire, although the fact that the names are the same seems unrelated to the Iron Age as Stanwick is derived from *stan* meaning "stone" and *wic* meaning "dwelling" or "hamlet" therefore a stone settlement.

6 April. Near to the bird feeding station a weasel rapidly dashed across the path. I assume it was a weasel because it was quite small and I glimpsed a white underside. Weasels can be differentiated from stoats because they don't have a black tail tip but this one moved too fast for me to check that. To tell the difference, a great friend of mine, Alan Reed, who sadly passed away several years ago, had an amusing but ultimately unhelpful saying. 'A weasel is weasily recognisable but a stoat is stoatally different.' The predatory weasels feed on small mammals and eggs, birds and small rabbits if rodents are scarce; they can kill efficiently when only eight weeks old.

An example of the mammal's occasional desperate predation occurred in May 2015 when an amateur photographer captured remarkable footage in a London park. A weasel had leapt on to a green woodpecker to kill it but the bird took flight with the weasel still on its back. Eventually, after flying about twenty metres, the bird landed, the weasel fell off and the woodpecker flew off escaping with its life.

***

Steve, a keen birdwatcher, told me that willow warblers, chiffchaffs, blackcaps, swallows and common terns have arrived; even an avocet has been spotted (I haven't seen any of these!). In the wildflower world bluebells, cowslips and brooklimes are appearing (I have seen these!]. When I met bird expert, Bob Webster, he told me the avocet had been on Tern Island and had only stayed for a couple of hours; later an avocet, presumably the same one, was seen further up the valley at Summer Leys Nature Reserve. Spring is picking up its pace!

**

I was reading John Craven's excellent and informative *Countryfile Handbook* and made an interesting discovery. The River Nene, our river, is at 148 miles, the third longest river in England with only the Thames (215 miles) and the Trent (185 miles) being longer. What about the Seven (220miles)? Well the source of that is at Plynlimon in Wales so it doesn't count. What about the Tweed (155 miles)? Part of that is in Scotland so that doesn't count either. So, discounting these two rivers of dual nationality our River Nene takes place third place just pipping the Great Ouse (143miles).

Another fact I have realised is that, as the River Nene bifurcates in Stanwick Lakes, then one branch meanders through the Nature Reserve before rejoining the main flow, the area occupied by the Visitor Centre and car park is actually an island surrounded by the river all sides. As I consider I have discovered this island:

I HEREBY CLAIM THIS LAND IN THE NAME OF GREAT BRITAIN AND HER MAJESTY, ELIZABETH, OUR QUEEN AND NAME IT NEWFOUNDLIZLAND IN HONOUR OF HER FORTHCOMING NINETIETH BIRTHDAY. GOD SAVE THE QUEEN. Hip hip hooray, hip hip hooray, etc.

I did place a small Union Jack on the island near the play area but some little kid nicked it.

***

12 April. Today we met a couple of Daves. First Dave Rees who immediately claimed he had seen a goldeneye, then Dave Goodier who said he had seen a kingfisher. It's very suspicious I told them that they only seem to have these sightings when they are on their own and never when they are with me. I teasingly said that their sightings could not be considered genuine as they had not been verified by a responsible and knowledgeable adult, i.e. me.

Next, we met Peter Davison trundling around the lakes on his tricycle; sometimes he peddles so slowly it is difficult to detect any forward movement. Although Pete has a few ailments, he always has a humorous tale to tell. His Professor Branestawm inspired vehicle has many appendages including a long black tube sticking up at the back like a rocket launcher but is actually where he keeps his crutches as he cannot walk very well. Whilst talking to him I pointed out that he seemed to have a flat tyre on one of his back wheels but, when he looked at it, he said it didn't matter because it was only flat at the bottom.

***

Bob Webster told me where the kingfishers were nesting so, a couple of times, I have crept to that location and found the two holes in the river bank. They are neat clean-cut apertures about three inches in diameter and smooth at the bottom where the birds have entered and exited. I looked around and didn't see a kingfisher but you will certainly know about it when I do.

13 April. Well, you didn't have to wait long; as I stood on the river bank opposite the nest site this morning I glimpsed bright blue on an old reed stalk: when I raised my binoculars the most rapid flash of the unmistakable colour passed before me. These are my poetic thoughts:

> *It takes patience to see the king,*
> *You need to be quiet and still,*
> *He's there on a branch o'er river flow,*
> *Lethal black beak ready to kill.*
> *Then straight down, a dart-like dive,*
> *A blue flash, a lightning streak,*
> *Before surfacing with fish, still alive,*
> *A small silver sliver in his beak.*

Once, there was a rather cruel custom in England and France of using the bodies of kingfishers as weathercocks. It was believed the direction of the wind, even indoors, could be determined by hanging the birds with wings spread, because the beak would always turn towards the wind. You'd have thought they could have just stuck a wet finger in the air.

Kingfishers were also known as "Halcyon birds" as it was believed they laid their eggs in the seven days either side of the winter solstice, this often being the warm spell in November known as an Indian summer. Actually, kingfishers usually lay their eggs in April or May.

14 April. Swans are nest building, but only one pair per lake following recent evictions of intruders. The construction is a slow meticulous process; the pen sits on her foundation pile of reeds then slowly and gracefully swings her head round from a pivot point at the base of her neck, sometimes to right behind her, before carefully selecting a reed which she swings back to the required position on the nest; she gently deposits it in place and nudges it to bed it in, before repeating the entire process. Her partner, the cob, is nearby and devotedly assists by tugging up suitable reeds and waddling over to place them on his beloved's building material pile.

***

A plant that is making its spring appearance is the hairy bittercress, a wildflower in the countryside and a weed in our gardens. It is a short unimpressive wiry plant with minute white flowers; the petals are about the size of a pinhead. Beneath the flowers are long thin seed pods which, when ripe, explode sending the seeds all around; each plant has about six hundred seeds with twenty in each pod. That is the reason they spread so quickly and are unwelcome in gardens. They grow almost anywhere, on open ground, on rocks, in walls and seem particularly partial to the joints of the brick paving on the drive of my house. However, they are plants with a split personality because, as well as being an annoying weed, they are also edible. They are of the same family as mustard and can be used in salads, soups or as a herb; they have a peppery, but not bitter, taste similar to rocket. If you fancy a try, just pull up the plant, cut off the root, discard any yellowish flowers or thickish stalks and it is ready to consume or cook. In the foragers' "bible", *Food for Free*, author, Richard Mabey, suggests, for a salad, mixing the leaves with those of dandelion, garlic mustard and charlock then dressing them with a mixture of sunflower oil and lemon juice. I haven't tried this for lunch as I prefer a bacon buttie.

19 April. The warmth today has awakened butterflies from their life as a pupa and I saw an orange tip delicately stretching its wings in the sun. Its appearance conveniently coincides with the flowering of its main larval food plants, lady's smock and garlic mustard (jack by the hedge). Also, in the past few days I have seen swallows and common terns for the first time this year.

21 April. Her Majesty's ninetieth birthday: I had planned to muster as many elderly dog walkers as I could into a column and march them round the lakes singing "God Save the Queen" but I couldn't persuade any of them to join me. So, I went on my own. To adopt a militaristic posture, I pushed my chest out as far as my arthritic back would allow then marched off swinging both arms vigorously (to the alarm of my dog whose lead I was still holding) singing "God Save the Queen",

"Rule Britannia", "Land of Hope and Glory" etc. at the top of my voice. Unfortunately, I don't possess a big bass drum.

When I returned to the car park I felt infused with nationalistic pride and patriotic fervour. However, my friends were concerned and, on their recommendation, I am seeing a psychiatrist next week.

22 April. Today we walked along the Nene Way on the other side of the river. Our dog, Caillou, likes this walk as he can be let off his lead. By the wood alongside the path there is some brooklime in flower. It has the wonderful scientific name of *veronica beccabunga* which sounds like a bit part character in Star Wars. The plant favours wet places and is the big sibling of common field speedwell – another film star, *veronica persica.* The blue flowers of the two plants are almost identical but brooklime grows taller and has larger leaves. Brooklimes are much visited by bees and today a solitary orange-tailed (*bombus lapidaries*) bumblebee dozily fusses around the flowers.

***

Today the sun doth permit the base contagious clouds to smother up his beauty from the world, that, when he please again to be himself, being wanted, he may be more wonder'd at, by breaking through the foul and ugly mist of vapours that did seem to strangle him. If the sun doth shineth every day to shine would be as tedious as to cloud; but when they seldom come, they wish'd for come, and nothing pleaseth but rare accidents.

Sorry about that paragraph based on a speech from the First Part of King Henry IV but it is the twenty-third of April, the four hundredth anniversary of the Bard's death in 1616, and all his stuff on the telly seems to have got to me.

Hearing or reading Shakespeare's words always stimulates me to write similar poetry.

The Bard's home was Stratford on Avon,
But, I've thought this time and again,
Although Stratford was his haven,
I wish it had been Stanwick on Nene.

My poem might not be quite as batty as it seems because I have discovered a Northamptonshire connection between the two rivers. The main source of the River Nene is near Arbury Hill but there is another tributary which rises at Naseby in Northamptonshire which is also the location of the source of the River Avon. So, after some diligent research I have found out what actually happened at the time of Shakespeare's birth.

One fine April day in 1562 Mary Shakespeare, who was with child, was sitting on the patio in the garden of her home in Stratford when she said to her husband, John, 'Gadzooks, John, luv, I fancieth a ride on the river.'

'Odds bodkins, pet, I will go and hireth us a punt.'

So, they set off up the Avon and several hours later

Mary piped up, 'Zounds, I now fancieth a saunter across yon green and pleasant land.'

After their ramble at Naseby, John thought it was time for them to be getting back home but when he came across the river unbeknownst to him it was the Nene and not the Avon.

'God's blood, luv, I couldn't findeth our punt so I have had to hireth another.'

As night began to fall they found themselves in unfamiliar surroundings, and Mary said, 'Forsooth, pet, I haveth chronic indigestion; it must be those pickled ferrets we had for lunch.'

'Donner und blitzen,' said John (running out of Shakespearian expletives) 'Mary, you are definitely going into labour, we must getteth thou to a place of rest immediately, toot sweet.' So, they made their way to the nearest settlement which happened to be Stanwick and on the outskirts they found an inn where, after several hours of painful contractions, Mary popped out her little lad, Willy.

Therefore, all references to Stratford-upon-Avon relative to Shakespeare's birth should be expunged from all historical documents and replaced with Stanwick on Nene as my version is based on accurate primary source material. For example, John Shakespeare's recipe for pickled ferrets is from the French culinary classic *Ye Very Laste Worde in Stake Flame Grilling* by Joan of Arc.

***

Among the birds I have seen recently is a drake shoveler on a lake consorting with a flock of tufted ducks, a pair of yellow wagtails flitting down the river and a chiffchaff perched atop a bush. The shoveler was easily recognisable by its long spatulate bill and its striking plumage of a dark green head, white breast and chestnut flank.

***

The weather continues to be exceptionally cold with temperatures rarely being above six degrees in the mornings; despite this, I have bravely (my wife says foolhardily) persisted and worn my shorts whilst dog walking all this month, mainly to please my lady fan base. I had hoped my legs would get a little browner but instead they have taken on a slightly purplish hue. Bob Monkhouse wittingly said, "They laughed when I said I wanted to be a comedian, well they're not laughing now." My version is, "They laughed when I said I was going to wear my shorts, well I'm wearing them and they're still laughing."

MAY

We have spent a couple of weeks on Anglesey and there have been a few very warm days while we were away, so, when we return to our Stanwick walks, we notice a significant difference. The grass, reeds and plants have shot up and foliage has thickened on the trees and shrubs. It is as though Act One of the year has finished and there has been a dramatic scene change ready for the next part of the performance.

***

Ne'er cast a clowt till May is out.

What does that actually mean? The first part is obvious and it is generally accepted to mean 'never discard [warm winter] clothing' but it is the second part which is ambiguous; does it mean until the month of May has ended or until the hawthorn is in bloom because May is another name for the hawthorn which flowers in late April or early May? There is also this ambiguity in many rhymes and Shakespeare's sonnet eighteen is a typical example

Rough winds do shake the darling buds of May,
And summer's lease hath all too short a date.

Did he mean the month or the tree?

However, there are similar sayings in other countries which definitely refer to the month; the French one is *En Avril ne te découvre pas d'un fil; en Mais fais ce qui te plait,* which translates as 'In April do not shed a single thread; in May do as you please.' Also, some lines from F. K. Robertson's 1855 Whitby Gazette tend to confirm the "month" definition.

So never think to cast a clout,
Until the month of May be out.

So, after that analysis, I favour the 'month' interpretation.

***

The hawthorn, in its alternative guise as the May tree, is the only tree named after the month in which it blooms. Also, it was previously known as the thorn tree and, as such, is the most common tree found in English place names, e.g. Thorne, Thornbury, Thornby, Thorncombe and Thorngumbald which couldn't be in anywhere else but Yorkshire. Its pretty blossom was once used extensively for decoration, but only outdoors as it was considered unlucky to bring it indoors. There is a bizarre but logical reason for this; the blossom contains the chemical trimethylamine which strangely is also a chemical found in decaying animal tissue. In former times bodies were kept in houses for several days prior to burial and they began to smell of this chemical, so it is not surprising that the same smell in the form of hawthorn blossom was unwelcome indoors.

12 May. The youngsters are arriving! On one of the lakes this morning we saw the first goslings of the year, a pair of newly born Canada geese youngsters in the company of their parents, one of which was leading and the other was at the rear checking that the infants didn't stray.

But Canada geese do not have a good press. In an article in the *Daily Mail*, journalist Robert Hardman described them as Britain's most hated bird after cooking expert, Prue Leith, was accused of breaking the law by making a Canada geese egg omelette. Apparently, she had contravened the Wildlife and Countryside Act of 1981 because you cannot take the eggs of a wild bird without having a sound ecological reason for doing so. Robert Hardman likened Canada geese to people who loaf around all day, claiming welfare benefits and being served ASBOs.

We have King Charles II to thank for their presence in this country (the Victorians are not the guilty party this time). He introduced them from North America to become ornaments in his London garden (St James's Park) and they soon became a craze amongst the nobility who all wanted them around their stately homes.

Here at Stanwick Lakes, the rangers attempt to control the population of Canada geese by pricking the eggs when they encounter them. Last year they dealt with around three hundred in this way.

14 May. Wildflowers are now appearing at a rate almost too numerous to record. However, here are some new arrivals I noticed on our walk this morning:

Red campion
Meadow buttercup
Wild Strawberry
Common vetch
Red clover
Dovesfoot cranesbill and its cousin, cut-leaved cranesbill
Common comfrey
Goatsbeard (this also has the folk name of "Jack Go to Bed at Noon" because its flowers have the habit of closing up at midday)
Lastly, my namesake, herb Robert

Also plentiful at the moment are the now ubiquitous rape plants which have escaped from controlled cultivation as their seeds have blown across the countryside; there hasn't been this much rape in England since the last Viking raids. The wildflower, charlock, is very similar to rape having almost identical flowers but more hairy leaves and stems; however, I haven't seen any for some time as it seems to have been swamped in the yellow swathes of rape.

15 May. It is Pentecost or Whit Sunday, which celebrates God and the Holy Spirit giving wisdom to people. In Gloucestershire Whit Sunday is called "bread and cheese day" because of an old custom of throwing bread and cheese. Doesn't everybody do that after a boozy dinner party?

At Kinewell Lake this morning there are yellow "seas" of buttercups and in other places tracts covered in the white global seed-heads of dandelion; they remind me of the countryside games we used to play as children. A buttercup flower would be placed under another child's chin and if it reflected yellow (it always did) it was proof they liked butter; today it would probably be olive oil based spread. The buttercup has a very good reason for being able to reflect this yellow UV light as it attracts pollinating insects, such as bees, whose eyes are sensitive to UV rays. The game played with dandelions was to tell the time by the number of blows of breath it took to remove the seeds; time-wise it was wildly inaccurate but I used to have a watch like that anyway. Also, young girls would spend ages making long chains of daisy flowers to hang round their necks.

A favourite pastime of boys was making "touch ovens". Someone always knew where clay could be found and news of the location rapidly spread. There, we would scoop out lumps of the moist, blue-grey stuff. It was then modelled into box shapes about eight inches long, four inches across and three inches deep – a description from those times demands imperial measurements; a small hole was then poked through one end. Some, more creative, boys even added lids with funnels. Next, touch wood had to be found; this was the soft, spongy dry wood from the trunks of dead trees and it was harvested like treasure by young lads. The wood was placed in the clay touch ovens and was lit – boys often carried boxes of matches – and it burned slowly with little flame but with billowing clouds of smoke. The objective was to race around the streets holding the touch oven aloft, leaving a long trail of smoke behind you often accompanying the action with impersonations of steam locomotive sounds. Eventually, the clay baked, the touch oven cracked and it was necessary to start again.

In those days in the 1940s and 50s groups of children would roam across the countryside, some little more than toddlers in the charge of older brothers or sisters, without thought or fear of danger, abduction, harm or abuse. The days were never long enough but the August school holidays seemed to last forever. They were golden, halcyon, Laurie Lee-esque times of utter happiness. I never envy the youngsters of today with their laptops, iPads, Xboxes etc. because I know with dazzling certainty they can never achieve the enjoyment we did from simple countryside pleasures.

***

On a hot day, a pair of red kites circle lazily in the sky then spiral upwards on the thermals like expertly piloted gliders; they break away, wheel down, find another thermal and start again. They are not hunting – this is just for fun! So beautiful, so effortless, so captivating! They remind me of Noel Harrison's song *Windmills of Your Mind* as they spiral in a never-ending circle.

Red kites are now a common sight in the skies over the Nene valley but for about a century they were absent from this country. They were driven to extinction at the end of the nineteenth century (bloody Victorians again!) mainly due to the invention of the breech-loading shotgun; they were reintroduced to this area in 1995 when thirty-five birds were brought from Spain to Fineshade Wood; later another thirty-four were introduced and since then they have spread so that now there are estimated to be eight or nine hundred red kites in east Northamptonshire and the surrounding area.

In Shakespearean times, red kites were a common sight in the skies over London but they had a reputation for stealing underwear from washing lines during the nesting season to use to line their nests. Eventually their numbers declined in the city; they were probably driven off by people desperate to get their knickers back. The Bard even refers to this habit of the red kite in *The Winter's Tale* when Autolycus says, 'When the kite builds, look to your lesser linen.'

20 May. I have been becoming increasingly concerned because, so far this year, I have not heard a cuckoo or seen a swift. In previous years I have experienced both long before now. However, I was relieved today to at least see a couple of swifts. Two people have told me they have heard a cuckoo in the last week including one man who said he had heard one at the lakes at twenty past five one morning; I'm prepared to make an effort to commune with nature but, for me, the cuckoos need to wait until later in the day.

April the fourteenth, St. Tiburtius Day, is traditionally the day cuckoos arrive in this country but this is usually first in the south west, often the Scilly Isles, before they move northwards. Incidentally, St. Tibutius was a Christian martyr who, in the third century, was buried, with Valerian and Maximus, on the fourteenth of April in the catacombs of Praetextatus on the Via Appia in Rome. He was converted to Christianity by his sister-in-law, Cecily [later St. Cecily] and when he was sentenced to death for his faith his executioner, Maximus, was so impressed with his courage and faith he too was converted, so he was also executed. Tiburtius must have had an extremely convincing evangelical sales pitch to persuade Maximus to join a movement he knew would result in his being killed. I'm not sure where the cuckoo became involved.

***

The seed heads of the dandelions have now almost all blown away leaving pathetic withered headless stems. The leaves of dandelions have long been known to be a diuretic and, in recognition of this, their French name is *pissenlit; en lit* means "in bed" so I will leave you to work out the meaning of the whole word.

***

On our walk by Mervyn's bench this morning we pass two of the Heritage Trail stones which mark the location of the Saxon, Norman and Medieval occupation of the site. Archaeological excavations at the northern end of Stanwick Lakes between 1985 and 1989 revealed the existence of the late Anglo-Saxon, Norman and Medieval settlement of West Cotton. The village comprised several groups of houses as well as gardens, streets, yards, paddocks, a manor house, a church and a watermill (no pub?); it was a community devoted to agriculture but the settlement was deserted by the mid-fifteenth century. It is believed the watermill was abandoned in the twelfth century because its water supply was disrupted by heavy flooding. Gradual desertion of the rest of the village followed, probably due to factors such as the Black Death but also possibly to the shift from arable to sheep farming that required larger areas of land for grazing.

The Heritage Trail stone markers, which help visitors appreciate the fascinating history of Stanwick Lake's past, were shaped and carved by apprentice stonemasons from Moulton College and the bronze resin plaques were made by sculptor, Neil Carter.

***

At the moment, there are flocks of grey lag geese of all ages wandering about on the paths and grass areas which are becoming covered in their squelchy dark green droppings. The herbage they feed on is quickly voided as it passes rapidly through their guts. The gatherings are like crèches with adults minding an equal number of goslings; the latter are of differing ages, some recently born, others larger and older. This gathering in flocks enables some to feed while others are on look-out for danger. At our approach, the adults shepherd the youngsters waddling into the lake to take refuge near the reeds. After we pass they return to their terrestrial vocation of grazing and defecating.

Grey lag geese (*anser anser*) are the ancestors of most of our domestic geese (*anser domesticus*) and they have been domesticated in this country since the fourteenth century. Since then many of the domesticated ones have become pure white. Grey lags are sometimes promiscuous and they have interbred with other species such as barnacle geese, Canada geese and even occasionally swans. There is also an ancient link to fertility; this survives in the nursery rhyme, "Goosey Goosey Gander" which has sexual overtones in its reference to "lady's chamber" and the sexual expression "to goose" is believed to derive from the rhyme.

The primary feathers of the left wing of grey lags were also used for quills as the feathers leaned away from the sight of right-handed writers.

22 May. We walk later on Sundays because I need to meet my Maker at eight o'clock at St Peter's to offload the sins I have stacked up during the week; so, when I walk at the lakes I feel pure and untainted; but it never lasts for long. However, today at quarter past eleven the Lord rewarded me for my attempts at virtue. My wife, Ann, and I stopped on a path in the woods: we listened: we turned and looked at each other: we both broke into a broad smile. We had just heard a cuckoo call for the first time this year. I said, 'You beauty, you absolute beauty!' Ann thought I was talking to her but I was referring to the cuckoo.

***

You may think that winter snows bring the year its time of whiteness but late May offers some competition. There are banks of hawthorn heavily adorned with its white blossom; lower, acres of the lacy heads of cow parsley – also known as Queen Anne's lace – are appearing and the white and yellow heads of the abundant ox-eye daisies are flowering; even the catkins of the pussy willows are turning into snowy balls of cotton wool. These, plus there are many other flowers of the same colour such as white campion, garlic mustard, white dead-nettle and the omnipresent daisy. Also, Tern Island is covered by hundreds of black-headed, but mainly white, gulls and the air above is full of their shrieking partners.

White is associated with goodness, innocence, purity, virginity and perfection. Wow, describes me to a T!

24 May. On the ground today we found an egg; it was almost ten centimetres across but, although it was whole in shape, the shell and "white" had been completely removed leaving just the yoke in its containing membrane. I gently poked it and found it was soft in places, harder in others. What creature, I wondered, could have removed this large egg from its nest, transported it some distance and then carefully removed the shell and "white" without disturbing the rest of it? – obviously, some creature with a large beak or mouth and surgical training.

26 May. The first cygnets have hatched. There are many nests around the lakes and we have been seeing the cobs and pens sitting on them for some time; they usually lay between five and seven eggs which hatch in thirty-five to forty days. Today one of the nests we had been watching was empty and a few minutes later we saw the family outing. The cob was following the pen and she had a couple of cygnets on her back, their little heads just poking above her wing feathers; three more youngsters were struggling up the pen's tail to clamber on board. Every time the mother bent forward and dipped her head into the water to feed, there was panic behind as the brood fought to cling on.

The cygnets remain with their parents for four or five months and don't breed themselves until they are about three years old. Swans can live for over twenty years.

To maintain my reputation for providing salacious facts, I wish to inform you that male swans are the only birds known to have a penis. I am not sure how the other birds cope or amuse themselves.

***

Snails are emerging from their dormancy to chomp their way through the countryside and our gardens. Their full title is the lengthy "terrestrial pulmonate gastropod molluscs" and most of them are common garden snails, *helix aspersa,* but our walking companion, Dave, says he has seen more of a different variety this year and when we are walking over the causeway he points some out to me; they have markedly darker rings on a creamier coloured shell and are brown-lipped snails, *cepaea nemoralis,* which are a favourite food of thrushes.

The slimy trail left by snails is from their foot which is a flat muscular organ; through this they secrete mucus which helps them move over rough surfaces by reducing friction.

There are always a lot of snails in our gardens because they multiply rapidly and can have over four hundred babies a year – so it will take you a very long time to eradicate them.

Snails can seal off the entrance to their shell and survive in suspended animation for several months. Also, they are hermaphrodites; this means they each have both male and female sex organs and can mate with themselves which must come in jolly handy during their long months of hibernation.

But we mustn't mock snails because scientists have discovered they are smarter than we previously believed and they can make complex decisions using just two brain cells; one of the cells tells the snail when it is hungry and the other when food is present. Remind you of anybody you know?

***

The last day of May: the sky is grit-grey, there is a strong, cold north-easterly blowing and the central heating and long trousers are back on.

JUNE

1 June. The first day of meteorological summer, and if that doesn't prove summerlike, it gets a second chance on the twenty-first when it is the first day of astronomical summer, but so far there is no sign of any decent weather or of June having an inclination to burst out all over.

If it's summer why isn't it warm because the sun is at its highest and the days their longest? This is due to an effect called Seasonal Temperature Lag. The earth absorbs heat energy from the sun and slowly releases it; however, water heats more slowly than land and at the start of summer the oceans are still cool from winter temperatures, so it is not until the oceans have been warmed up and started to release their heat that the atmosphere warms up; therefore, we usually get our highest temperatures in late July and August.

***

Have you ever been walking on the bank of a slow flowing stream at this time of year and noticed something bright blue flash before your eyes? I am not referring to a kingfisher this time but something much smaller. It was probably a banded agrion, a member of the damselfly family. These attractive dragonfly-like insects have thin metallic blue bodies and the males have transparent bluish wings with a round dark mark on them. However, as is often the case, the females are less attractive and are a dull green all over but they more than make up for their dowdiness by their productivity; when suitably primed they lay ten eggs per minute for forty-five minutes.

Today, whilst walking along the river I found a banded agrion which seemed to be entangled in the long grass; I gently pinched its wings between my fingers and released it into the air.

One evening some years ago I was strolling along the bank of the River Ise near Finedon and found several scatterings of banded agrion wings on the path; the insects had been caught in flight by birds or bats, their bodies devoured, the wings discarded and they had played their role in nature's food chain.

Also flying near streams at the moment are common blue damselflies which are often seen in pairs; these have blue bodies with thin black bands around them. They mate by the male holding the female by her neck while she turns her lower body round to his reproductive tackle. Do not try this at home.

***

It is a beautiful but quiet time of year in many respects, beautiful because the vegetation is lush and the trees are almost fully dressed, quiet because the lushness is like a curtain concealing the activity on the stage behind. We hear many small birds but don't see them and we haven't seen a deer for weeks; (retrospective comment: such is the unpredictability of nature, we saw a deer the day after writing this.) they are all too busy attending to their offspring.

Today the second of June, we did however see a grey heron, the first one for some time. It was on a fishing trip from a nearby heronry, probably the one at the Titchmarsh Nature Reserve a few miles down the valley. Herons travel as far as forty kilometres from home in search of food.

Herons lay between two and seven of their pale greenish blue eggs on a high treetop nest, usually in late March, and with an incubation period of twenty-three to twenty-eight days and a fledging time of forty-two to fifty-five days the chicks are now at their most hungry and demanding.

***

However, there are some creatures that are plenteous after recent rains – slugs – mainly the large black ones, *arion ater*. These move in the same way as snails by rhythmic waves of muscular contractions of their feet and they have two pairs of tentacles on their heads, the top ones for seeing and the lower ones for smelling. The reason they are mainly active after rain is because their bodies are mostly liquid and they have to generate mucus to survive; in dry weather, they retreat to damp places. The slime trail they leave has many uses; it helps them recognise the trail of others of the same species, enables them to track a mate and find their way home. The mucus on their bodies also makes it harder for predators to pick them up and hold them but they are still preyed upon by every vertebrate group. Apart from their sliminess, to defend themselves they also contract their bodies and stubbornly attach themselves to the surface beneath.

But, as gardeners know, they feed on almost any plant material; each average UK garden is estimated to be home to about 20,000 of the blighters.

Because they are quite repugnant, not many poets have turned their pens to writing about slugs so I have composed my own verses.

Is it possible to love a slug,
Just pick it up and give it a hug?
Or is that taking things too far?
And you're better keeping the thing in a jar,
Where you could look at it all day long,
And maybe sing it this little love song,
'Dear slug our love can never be,
You're just a bit too yucky for me.'

Wait a minute, I've now learned something new,
Instead of one sex organ, slugs have two,
And the potential here is really great,
For the various ways how we could mate,
But the offspring of our coupling, we'd find in time,
Would be six feet long and covered in slime.

7 June. The first shorts and T-shirt walk of the summer. Next to the small lake at the far end from the Visitor Centre, there is a patch of ragged robin growing and it is the only place I have seen it at the Lakes. This pretty flower is declining due, sadly, to human activity such as land drainage, and loss of ponds and wet meadows.

Ragged robins are related to the campion family and have flowers that look as though they have been through a shredder. Their name is apt as the pink petals are like tiny tattered rags of cotton.

In his poem, *Idylls of the King* Tennyson likened a pretty damsel in ragged attire to the plant.

> *And should some great court-lady say, the prince*
> *Hath pick'd a ragged robin from the hedge,*
> *And like a madman brought her to the court.*

Maintaining a romantic theme, in former times men carried ragged robin in their pockets as it was believed it would make them successful in love. Also, girls would give ragged robin plants the names of village boys and the one that flowered first would bear the name of the boy the girl would marry – an early version of online dating.

The botanical name of ragged robin is *lychnis cuculi,* the *lychnis* coming from the Greek word for "lamp" because the pink flowers stand out in a green landscape and *cuculi* means cuckoo because this is another plant whose flowering coincides with the arrival of that bird.

***

At the height of summer, the river near the old railway bridge is often teeming with fish but they haven't arrived yet. However, I have now seen a chub with its open white-lipped mouth facing upstream.

We check to see what's in the river every time we cross the bridge. Some time ago Ann reached the bridge before me and looked into the water. 'Quick Bob,' she called but I arrived too late; she had seen an otter which had stuck its head out of the water, looked at her, then dived under and away before I could get there. Other people have told me they have seen otters; one man said he watched one swim across a large lake; another person saw a pair in the river near the entrance pedestrian bridge; dog-walker Helen watched one with two cubs near the river lock.

In his *Countryfile Handbook* John Craven gives some tips for otter-spotting: it's best to go out at dawn or dusk when they are feeding: leave your furry friend at home as otters would flee if they smelt a dog: Mr. Craven also says you can smell their presence and they have been described as smelling like jasmine tea, lavender or new mown hay which seems a bit confusing as these things all smell quite different.

***

The Mysterious Things in the Lake.

'Look, Bob, what's that over there?' Dave said as we were crossing the causeway about eight o'clock in the morning. I trained my binoculars where he was pointing;

there was a dark object in the lake surrounded by roiling and splashing water; it was about a metre across, a hundred metres from the bank and in a shallow area of the lake.

'It seems like some dead creature floating on the water and fish are feasting on it and tearing it apart,' I speculated.

'There's another… and another… and another,' Dave said and then added that he could see about five of them so I discounted the dead creature theory. Whatever they were, they were now moving across the surface and I made my second speculation.

'They could be mink feeding because there must be hundreds of newly hatched fish in there.' I continued to watch the shapes. 'But I can't see any heads popping out of the water,' so theory two was also discounted. Then one of the shapes surfaced nearer the bank and, on top of a blackish tubby form, a fin flicked up. 'They're fishes!' I concluded and we continued to discuss the sighting as we carried on walking.

Back home I leafed through my nature guidebooks then Googled the phenomenon and discovered the fish were tench. At this time of year, the males chase the females and clamber on their backs to mate, and they do this in the shallows of soft bottomed lakes.

10 June. It's the Queen's ninetieth birthday again today but I am not marching round the lakes singing this time; instead, to celebrate the event, I am wearing my Union Jack underpants. I have decided to also have a second "official" birthday in the future and when I discussed it with my family they said it was a good idea but asked if I wouldn't mind if they didn't get involved. Anyway, I enquired about hiring St Paul's cathedral for my celebration, just like the Queen's, but unfortunately, they don't allow discos so maybe I'll forget the whole thing and just dog-walk round the lakes as usual.

***

I'm a technophobe so I leave it to Ann to master the trappings of modern technology. Today I called on her expertise with her Smartphone to take a picture of a large dragonfly that was resting on the path. It was about five centimetres long with yellow and black stripes along its abdomen. At home, with the help of the Smartphone image, I identified it as a female black-tailed skimmer. Dragonflies are divided into two groups, hawkers and darters, and the black-tailed skimmer is in the latter category which prefers to sit on an observation perch then dart out to catch prey; the hawkers just fly around searching for quarry.

Black-tailed skimmers are a relatively recent arrival on our shores, the first one having been recorded in 1934, but they have multiplied and become common mainly due to the creation of gravel pits which provide the waterside areas of open vegetation they prefer.

***

Beware there's danger about! Two poisonous plants are now flowering, foxglove and hemlock. Last week, near the car park at Kinewell Lake, there were two foxgloves in flower, this week there were ten. Foxglove (*digitalis purpurea)* is a beautiful tall plant with tubular bell-like flowers which have a spotted interior; as we looked at one flower a bee disappeared completely inside. The whole plant is poisonous due to the presence of *digitalis* but the leaves have a beneficial use as medication for heart failure; however, consumed in excess, it leads to cardiac arrest. My Collins Gem *Wild Flowers* book, which I carry with me on my walks at this time of year, wittingly states, "Foxglove is the source of the drug digitalis which is used for the treatment of human heart conditions (physical ones, not psychological ones!)." So, admire the plant's beauty but NEVER be tempted to consume any part of it.

Hemlock is an umbellifer like cow parsley but it grows much taller and has purple-spotted stems. It is a very poisonous plant and its stem juice kills by paralysing the nervous system causing respiratory failure. People who have been poisoned by it have usually mistaken it for other plants such as parsley or carrot leaves. Seventeen people were poisoned in Italy after shooting and eating small wild birds which had fed on the plant. Did I hear someone say, "serve 'em right"? Hemlock was also famously used to kill the Greek philosopher Socrates.

I could give a recipe for making a phial of the potion but I am concerned it might result in me being an accessory to the need for a future exhumation.

Not only have the cuckoos arrived but also the cuckoo spit. These frothy saliva-like blobs which are appearing on plants are nothing to do with birds expectorating but are the deposits of the nymphs of the froghopper insect, *aphrophora spumaria;* the insect is also known as the spittle bug, frog spit and snake spit. The froth insulates the nymphs against heat and cold, and also protects them from predators. They pump the sap of plants into their stomachs through their snouts then exude it as small bubbles through their anuses, which makes me think they would be a popular novelty act on *Britain's Got Talent.*

The nymphs are four millimetres long, green frog-like bugs and when they emerge as froghoppers they are capable of incredible gymnastic feats; another reason Simon Cowell would love them on his show. They can jump seventy centimetres vertically and a hundred times their own length horizontally; furthermore, they leap with 400 g's of acceleration; so what, you might think, but to put this into perspective a jet pilot would black out at a mere 9 g's. (g is a unit of stress measurement for bodies undergoing acceleration).

So, it's a "yes" from me!

17 June. National Flip Flop Day in the United States: I don't know why they feel they need a day to celebrate those strappy things; I tripped and fell flat on my face when I tried to wear a pair. However, the thought of all those ghastly bare feet reminded me of a plant sometimes called granny's toenails because of its claw-like seedpods. It is mostly called birdsfoot trefoil, the first part being named after the seed pods and the second from the leaves which have five leaflets, two of which are bent back leaving three prominent protruding ones, hence trefoil.

Due to the black seedpod "claws" the plant was once associated with evil as they were likened to the devil's claws.

Here are some of the more than seventy local names that birdsfoot trefoil has, as well as granny's toenails:

Grandmother's slippers

King's fingers

Cat's claws

Crow's feet

God Almighty's thumb and finger (the French name for the flower is *pied du mon dieu*)

Ladies fingers and the thumbs

And the most common one in this area, "eggs and bacon". I have now begun my search for the fried bread plant.

***

There is a flower I have been passing regularly but have taken little notice of, assuming it to be some sort of clover because the flowers have tightly packed round heads. However, these are yellow with orange tips and my research has revealed they are not clovers but kidney vetch, *anthyllis vulneraria,* also known as woundwort or ladies' fingers. This is a medicinal plant, *vulneraria* means "wound healer", and it was an ancient remedy for minor wounds, cuts and bruises. There is quite a variety in the flower's colours and shapes because it has twenty sub-species, five of which are found in the UK. It makes an important contribution to the ecology because it is the sole food of the larvae of the small blue butterfly which is in serious decline.

It flowers from June to September and the only place I have seen it so far this year is along the causeway.

But this kidney vetch is not even a member of the vetch, *vicia,* family which are completely different plants. The main varieties flowering at the moment are tufted vetch and common vetch; these have purple flowers and pinnate leaves on opposite sides of stalks with curly tendrils at the ends which the plants use to clamber up adjacent vegetation; occasionally they even "strangle" smaller plants. The two differ in that the flowers of common vetch grow in pairs whereas those of the tufted vetch are in dense clusters.

Actually, we shouldn't allow the definition of "vetch" to be restricted by botanical categories because "vetch" is an ancient English word meaning any plant grown for silage or fodder.

20 June. Whilst walking through the woods near Tern Island Lake, we met Jane coming in the opposite direction. She stopped about fifty metres from us, shortened Barney's lead and pointed to something by the side of the path in front of her. Through my binoculars, I saw the distinctive red cap and yellow rump of a green woodpecker. It was a fledgling which hadn't fully mastered the art of flight. Ann also shortened Caillou's lead and we could advance to within a metre of the bird which just did a few hops. The piercing, staring eye in its black face gave it a terrified appearance. Then we heard a shrill laugh-like call overhead as a parent passed over.

We could do nothing to help, and left the youngster in the hope that the parent would come to its aid, and the chick wouldn't fall prey to the rawness of nature. There was a similar occurrence the following day when Dave, ahead of me, stopped and pointed to a bird on the path about thirty metres in front. My binocular vision revealed it to be a jay, a bird we don't see often at the Lakes. It soon disappeared into the trees as we walked forward.

**

Here's a way to amuse any small children you may have with you on your walk – or grandchildren – or in the case of my generation probably great grandchildren. First, you have to ask your little ones whether they believe in pixies; if they do, OK, but if they don't you need to employ some imaginative persuasion to convince them of pixies' existence.

Next, you need to find a white dead-nettle; these have leaves the same as stinging nettles but don't sting. Then look for a cluster of white flowers around the stem.

Question time: ask your little companions if they would like to see where pixies hide their slippers. Finally, turn over the white dead-nettle flowers and, surprise! there are the pointed little shoes. If you are certain you have found the right plant, you can even show the children how to suck the honey-tasting nectar from the flower.

If the youngsters are not amused take them home to play with their Xboxes.

23 June. In, out, in, out, no I'm not practising the hokey cokey but trying to decide which way to vote in today's EU referendum. Anyway, at Stanwick Lakes we are doing our bit for *entente cordiale* because we currently have a French ranger, Louis, who is here on a twelve weeks' work placement from a college in Toulouse. At least, his name's not Dave!

24 June. Custer Cameron's Last Stand. On this day in 1876 (2016), native American warriors (UK electorate) led by chiefs Crazy Horse (Nigel Farage) and Sitting Bull (Boris Johnson) defeated the US army (Remain campaigners) commanded by Lt-Col George Custer (David Cameron) in a battle (referendum) at Little Bighorn (polling stations).

Some lines from G. K. Chesterton's poem *The Secret People* convey the rebellious mood of the nation at the time of the referendum:

> *We hear men speaking for us of new laws strong and sweet,*

Yet there is no man speaketh as we speak in the street.

It may be we shall rise the last as Frenchmen rose the first.

Our wrath come after Russia's wrath and our wrath be the worst.

It may be we are meant to mark with our riot and our rest

God's scorn for all men governing. It may be beer is best.

But we are the people of England; and we have not spoken yet.

Smile at us, pay us, pass us. But do not quite forget.

(I love the end of that sixth line!)

However, I take comfort in that, no matter what social and economic turmoil and squabbling is going on in the political world, life in nature, Stanwick Lakes in particular for me, carries on unaffected by it all.

June the twenty-fourth is also St John's Day and a plant that traditionally flowers on that day is perforate, or common, St John's wort; this year I saw the first one on the twenty-sixth of June. The plant exudes a blood red liquid from its stem which, in ancient times, was considered to represent the blood of St John the Baptist after his murder. The plant's botanical name is *hypericum perforatum*, the *hypericum* being derived from the Greek *hyper* meaning "above" and *eikon* meaning "picture" which is from the ancient Christian tradition of placing the plant over icon images on St. John's Day to ward off evil spirits.

The pretty flower is called perforate because the leaves appear to have minute holes in them, you might need a magnifying glass to see them, and the five-petalled yellow flowers have tiny black spots. Because of the belief that the plant drives away evil spirits, it has long been used as a herbal remedy to relieve melancholy and depression. The flower's evil-bashing qualities are described in this poem from around 1400.

St John's wort doth charm all witches away
If gathered at midnight on the Saint's holy day,
Any devils or witches have no power to harm
Those that gather the plant for a charm.
Rub the lintels with that red juicy flower;
No thunder or tempest will then have the power
To hurt or hinder your house; and bind
Round your neck a charm of similar kind.

***

Water rails are secretive, rarely seen, birds which spend most of their existence sneaking around in the bottom of reed beds, and their presence is only betrayed by their piglet-like squeaks and grunts. So, we were surprised to see a juvenile wandering around in the open near a flock of about fifty grey lag geese. However, it is common at this time of year for the offspring of many species, which have only recently learned to walk or fly, to be found venturing out wondrously discovering the wide world and being naively unaware of the dangers they face.

We walked on and left the young water rail to whatever nature had planned for it.

30 June. Summer hasn't arrived yet. It has been cool, cloudy and showery for the last three weeks.

JULY

1 July. On this day last year, the temperature was thirty-five degrees; today it is fifteen.

Aren't great crested grebes brilliant? Like elegant fashion models they glide through the water; their long necks and coiffured ruffs and crests would attract media attention at Ascot's Ladies' Day. They can dance too, and perform a graceful *pas de deux* at mating time, facing each other and shaking their heads from side to side. Another of their balletic performances is the "reed dance"; pairs both dive to the lake bed where they collect a beak-full of reeds. After surfacing, they arc their necks down and forwards so their heads are almost touching the water; they then swim rapidly towards each other and, on meeting, they tread water furiously so their bodies rise almost vertically, before lovingly presenting their reed-gifts to their mates.

However expert and graceful they are in water, they are clumsy on land, their bodies not being designed for walking because their legs are positioned too far back. In water, this enables them to adopt a torpedo-like shape with their heads, necks and bodies stretched out and their legs at the back performing as propeller engines. They usually lay two eggs and the young are capable of swimming and diving soon after hatching. These youngsters, being fluffy with black and white stripes, are totally unlike their parents and it is difficult to believe they will eventually morph into adult great crested grebes.

At this time of year, they are performing another of their tricks; they carry their chicks on their backs, their little heads just peeping above their parents' wing feathers, and looking around like kids on a fairground ride. Often the adults dive under leaving the youngsters on the surface worrying they have been orphaned, but the parents soon return so they can clamber back on board.

In the nineteenth century, great crested grebes were almost hunted to extinction (those bloody Victorians again!) so their head plumage could be used to decorate hats; it is estimated that only about thirty-two pairs remained in Europe, but fortunately a protection programme was started and numbers recovered. It's a surprise any wildlife was still about when Edward VII ascended to the throne in 1901.

Here is my tribute to great crested grebes in July:

Who coiffured your stylish crown?
Elegant, diving, dancing bird,
Carefully tending to every tuft,
Till crest and ruff perfection reached,
Admiring glances to attract,
Adoration turned to love.

What secrets are found beneath the tide?
Elegant, diving, dancing bird,
What food fare for your fluffy young?
Who wait abandoned by your dive,
Then clamber on your surfaced back,
Returned to safety, parental love.

Your courting dance has long since passed,
Elegant, diving, dancing bird,
When, with your lover face to face,
Your head from side to side you shook,
Displaying "no" but meaning "yes",
Returning loyalty and love.

Next your reed dance you performed,
Elegant, diving, dancing bird,
From deep you brought your gift of love,
And rose up proudly face to face,
Hoping that your marshy gift,
Returned, would ever be, with love.

6 *July*. The wildflowers are now rioting; the July shift is clocking on and the early starters are beginning to wither; the upright hedge parsley is replacing the fading cow parsley. When admiring the pretty pink flowers on the dog rose, look out for a bright red woolly fibrous growth on the shrub; this is Robin's pincushion and it is not part of the shrub at all but a parasitic growth, a gall, caused by the Bedeguar wasp. This four millimetres long black insect lays its eggs in the buds of the dog rose and the gall

is produced when the larvae hatch and form their own chamber. There can be as many as fifty chambers in each gall and the larvae overwinter in them before emerging as wasps in the summer. These galls are not common and I have only found about six this year.

Our ancestors were fascinated by anything unusual like Robin's pincushion and convinced themselves they must have medicinal benefits. Here are some of the remedies they placed faith in.

In Sussex in the 1860s, Robin's pincushion was hung around the neck as a cure for whooping cough.

In Shropshire in the 1880s, it was hung on the chest as a remedy for toothache.

In Wiltshire at the end of the nineteenth century, it was carried in a pocket to cure rheumatism.

At the same period in Wales, it was placed under a pillow to prevent insomnia.

My favourite is this; in mid-nineteenth century Northamptonshire it was placed in a coat cuff turn-up to prevent the wearer being flogged. Trust Northamptonshire lads to get themselves into a situation where they needed to do something to reduce the prospect of their being thrashed instead of using Robin's pincushion to cure an ailment. Anyway, if I'd have known about this when I was a schoolboy, I would have thought it worth trying because I received several canings at my school in Wellingborough for misdemeanours I couldn't possibly tell you about.

O.K., I'll relate just one:

At mid-morning break we were given a small bottle

of milk and these bottles were kept in crates at the bottom of some steps next to the subterranean kitchens; two prefects stood next to the crates to hand out the bottles.

Before the break there had been some athletics on the school field which everyone watched. At the given end-of-session signal we all raced down the playground to get our milk. I arrived first and the pushing of the mob behind sent me stumbling downwards knocking the two prefects flying. They claimed I had done it deliberately so I was taken to the Headmaster and despite my protestations of innocence I was given "six of the best".

Amazingly, last year at an Old Boys' reunion luncheon, nearly sixty years after my caning, I was talking to a chap who said, 'Do you remember that time you got the cane for knocking those prefects over?'

'Of course I do,' I replied.

'It wasn't your fault, was it? I was behind and saw what happened.'

I smiled and thought *it's a pity you didn't say anything in my defence at the time.*

I didn't buy him a pint!

Finally, who on earth is this guy Robin who has a pastime which involves the need for a pincushion? I suspect it could be Robin Hood because he wore tights and that natty little green hat with a feather in it. This is confirmed by a conversation overhead several centuries ago in Sherwood Forest.

Robin Hood: Friar Tuck, be a darling and pass me my equipment please.

Friar Tuck: Yes sir, do you mean your bow, arrows and quiver?

Robin Hood: No, you fool, my pincushion. I am pinning up the hem of some curtains I am working on.

Friar Tuck: If you don't mind my saying, sir, the way you are going you would make a lovely wife for the Sheriff of Nottingham and that might be your best way of defeating him.

Robin Hood: You cheeky bugger!

(Friar Tuck rapidly exits left, as Robin Hood throws his knitting needles at him).

***

Because of the recent humid and showery weather, the vegetation has grown higher and more densely than usual. The swathe of hemlock along the riverbank is reaching rainforest proportions; I am six feet tall and plants like rosebay willow herb, teasel and Himalayan balsam tower over me.

This was emphasised recently when we went to look for the kingfisher and its nest hole in the riverbank; we walked along the pedestrian and disabled persons' boardwalk towards the tree house hide then through the long grass to the river, but when we got there we couldn't even see the river because of the high vegetation. I would have needed a machete to thrash my way through. So, we had to abandon our expedition and turn back.

***

Nature in the raw continues to be red in tooth and claw. We found a dead swift on the path by the play area; it was a sad sight but interesting to be able to examine a swift closely: next we came across a baby rabbit at Kinewell Lake with a bloody wound on its neck; at first, we thought it was dead, but it twitched a leg and opened an eye; however, we realised it didn't have a future so I nudged it into the longer grass with my trekking pole and left it. The following day it was a dead juvenile common gull we came across which had a gory gash on its throat; yesterday there was a scattering of feathers on the path and in the nearby grass a pair of clawed-feet legs and two grey and white wings surrounded by splatters of blood; something had consumed the body. All these are upsetting to find but part of nature's scheme we must accept.

We usually think this aspect of nature is confined to the vertebrates but the plant world can also be brutal and ruthless in its determination to survive – just without the blood and screaming. Plants such as butterbur with their elephant ear-like leaves deny sunlight to surrounding vegetation causing it to wither or struggle to thrive. Other plants that have tendrils such as white bryony, bindweed and tufted vetch clamber up and all over other flowers strangling the life from them. Rapidly growing and very abundant species like Himalayan balsam and fleabane squeeze out surrounding growth by their sheer volume and density.

The rawness of nature was brought home to me recently; actually, it was brought home to the garden of my home. We have a small vegetable patch purely for the pleasure of being able to bring some fresh summer produce to the table. However, there is a flock of house sparrows which frequent some nearby trees and they believe they have an entitlement to share our food; often, when I have gone down the garden about thirty of them have flown up from the vegetables. So, our solution was to spread a net across the plants and this prevented the birds from feeding on the tender shoots, but the recently arrived fledglings are not very smart because they flutter down and get entangled in the net. I had to quickly disentangle one the other day before our Westie, Caillou, could get to it, but yesterday there were two netted up and, as Ann was releasing one and before she could stop him, Caillou had grabbed the other little bird in his mouth. Alerted by Ann's scream, I raced (hobbled!) down and prised open the dog's mouth to release the chick but it was already dead; there wasn't any blood so I don't know whether it died of shock or by being crushed.

We were upset, not only for the death of the bird, but because our dear, adorable, (spoilt), butter-wouldn't-melt-in-its-its-mouth little dog had killed, but that's what Westies are trained to do as they were developed for hunting and ratting. So, we forgave him as his actions were instinctive.

Now the net has been removed because we decided the life of small birds is more precious than the quality of our salads. The sparrows again use our garden as their supermarket and, as I watch them scurrying amongst the lettuce, I am reminded of author Peter Robinson's apt description of them in one of his DCI Banks books as mice with wings.

12 July. I had two country walks today. In the evening, Ann was helping the local Cub pack during their cycle ride at the lakes, so I took the opportunity to also go there and have a walk. My first objective, in the hope of spotting an otter, was to stroll slowly and silently along the river bank in the John Craven recommended manner, that is, alone, in the evening and without a dog, but no matter how stealthily I edged beside the reeds I didn't see much other than a few swans and mallards; also, it was raining so that had driven most wildlife into shelter.

My second objective was to see what interesting wildflowers were now growing along Marsh Lane. Disappointingly, when I got there the complete lane – the grassy stone road and the wide verges either side – had been brutally mown down to stubble. Luke, the head ranger, told me the next day that the Environment Agency was responsible; they had flattened the area to maintain access to the river locks. Obviously, the Environment Agency is not always sensitive to the environment and I wondered if they had complied with the Wildlife and Countryside Act 1981 by taking measures to ensure that they didn't disturb any wild bird while it was nesting; this law applies throughout the nesting season from the first of March to the thirty-first of August. It is a dilemma country workers face; at the time of year when vegetation has grown to its thickest and needs cutting back the workers are restrained by the requirement to protect wildlife.

The only notable sightings I had that evening was a tree with eight little egrets roosting in it, and a solitary round-shouldered heron hunched over the water like a grey old man surveying his allotment.

Also, I did discover two hazel trees sumptuously adorned with green nuts; I am not prepared to tell you where this is, but I will be passing that way in a couple of months with a plastic bag in my pocket.

As the sky darkened there was a coterie of black-coated cormorants on a spit of land at the end of a lake island; they occasionally fanned out their wings to a heraldic posture as though having a bored yawn.

I met Ann back at the car park where the Cubs were having a break from cycling and were swarming over the play area equipment; the Cubs were the most interesting mammals I had seen all evening.

14 July. Usually our visits to the lakes are very happy but today it was sad.

We often meet Trish and Denise with their dogs Skye and Tiana; Skye is a "lady" Westie which we call Caillou's girlfriend. The two Westies love to meet, stand nose to nose then romp playfully around each other. Skye refuses to walk if she senses Caillou in the area and she pulls Trish towards him.

Today I saw Trish and Denise getting out of their car and Trish walked quickly and solemn-faced towards us. Immediate reaction – where was Skye? Tearfully Trish told us that Skye had been unwell last week, she had taken her to the vets, spleen cancer was diagnosed and darling, cute Skye had to be put to sleep. It was tears all round as we hugged Trish to comfort her.

We hope she will soon get a puppy replacement and we will see her on her usual walks round the lakes.

16 July. Halfway through the month and there are still no regular signs of summer. Dear Helios, god of sun, you've probably been away on holiday or something but we really need you to get busy as summertime is running out.

***

I had been concerned about the lack of butterflies this summer then I heard an item on the radio news which said there was a shortage due to the poor spring and early summer weather. Now, fortunately Helios, the god of sun, has answered my prayer and we are having the hottest and sunniest spell of the year. This has encouraged the butterflies to emerge so I have been concentrating on observing them. In the last few days I have seen small whites, small tortoiseshells, ringlets, red admirals, speckled woods and meadow browns. The orange tips I noticed some weeks ago have now gone; they usually hatch, fly, lay their eggs then disappear before the month of July.

There is ample food for the butterflies at the moment, their main source being nectar from flowers but they will also feast on fruit juices and the fluid from decaying flesh, muddy puddles and dung; so, they can't be all that fussy!

I am hoping to spot something more unusual than the common ones and with around five thousand species of butterflies and moths in Europe I reckon my chances are quite good.

There are some broad guidelines for distinguishing between butterflies and moths but there also many exceptions that don't conform to these rules. Generally, butterflies are day-fliers and rest with their wings closed above their backs, whereas moths are mostly nocturnal and settle with their wings out to the side. Also, butterflies have a small knob on the end of their antennae and moths have feathery antennae.

Due to the considerable similarity between butterflies and moths, many European languages make no distinction between them; in French a butterfly is a *papillon diurnes,* a day butterfly, and a moth is a *papillon nocturnes,* a night butterfly. Incidentally, *papillon* is also a nickname for a parking ticket and, in *amour,* the verb *papilloner* describes the action of a promiscuous person who switches from one lover to another like a butterfly flits between flowers.

Two caterpillars were sitting on a branch when a butterfly passed overhead. One caterpillar said to the other, 'You'd never get me up in one of those.'

21 July. Regarding summer: Is that it then – the statutory three hot days and a thunderstorm?

***

The thousands of screeching black-headed gulls have vacated Tern Island; they have taken their noisy, recently fledged kids to the council rubbish dump for a crash course on scavenging. So now, other birds are reoccupying the island, among them ducks, geese, oystercatchers and some cormorants. A pair of magpies is pecking over the deserted nesting sites for tasty egg fragments and other detritus left by the gulls and terns.

For their nests, the gulls scoop a hollow in the ground and line it with reeds and twigs; these nests are often only about one metre apart so, on a densely gull-populated space like Tern Island, there is little space for vegetation to thrive; but now the birds have gone the plants are flourishing helped also by the bird droppings which have nourished the soil. The mauve flowers of willow herb are dominant.

I have concluded that cormorants are not well designed; their necks are quite reptilian and too long, their tails are too short and their wings set too far back in their bodies. They are gawky on land and have a torpedo shape when flying, the same as they have when diving; they swim through the air and fly underwater, but it is to the latter that they are best adapted as they can spend up to two minutes fishing beneath the lakes. Also, they are elitist, standing in groups on the end of islands aloof from other birds. In their black plumage, they remind me of clubbable, old fashioned gentlemen discussing superior matters; they seriously need to be able to smoke pipes.

Cormorants were originally coastal birds and were first recorded nesting inland as recently as 1981, but they have adapted well to this habitat and are now common on many lakes.

***

On one of the recent hot and humid days, there was an unusual and initially inexplicable phenomenon. Hundreds of gulls were assembling in the sky and circling around, not in unison but individually; they were spread out across the cloudless blue and more were arriving from all directions. I watched them for several minutes trying to understand what they were doing and what was attracting them.

I looked down to think what the reason could be and saw the answer before me. There were several flying ants crawling about and I remembered that on a particular sultry, sweltering day swarms of winged queen and reproductive male ants erupt from their underground nests and spiral skywards like columns of smoke. The gulls I had observed were feasting on them; it must be a tasty dietary change from council tip scraps.

***

The wildflowers are now in their full glory. The banks of the causeway have the greatest variety and no cottage garden could match the colours and diversity of the plants along there: domed dazzlingly bright yellow heads of yarrow: large white bindweed flowers dotted everywhere: purple spearheads of the woundworts: mauves and pinks of willow herbs, both great and rose-bay varieties: black and purple knob-heads of black knapweed. However, there is one less attractive flower, gipsywort; this plant has jagged nettle-like leaves and small white flowers positioned up the stem tucked into the base of the leaves.

Gipsywort is the original fake tan as the juice of the plant was once used as a cosmetic to darken the skin. It gets its name because Romany people were supposed to have used it for this purpose and also that gipsy fortune-tellers dyed their clothes black with it. The fact that particularly endears the plant to me is that it smells of gin and tonic when crushed so I'll be having a whiff of gipsywort this evening when the sun is over the yardarm.

27 July. Caillou is not walking with us at the moment; he has been prescribed a week's rest. He had started to become reluctant to go up and down steps and stairs seeming to have a problem with one of his back legs. So, we took him to see the vet and, after a thorough examination, she diagnosed that movement in his rear left hip was restricted. We are hoping this is a temporary condition and not due to arthritis; at least the baby house sparrows will be safe for a while. Anyway, he had a painkilling injection and we have to give him some medication for a week. However, our son is on holiday now so we are dog-sitting his Bichon Frise, Rockie, and taking her on our morning walks. Caillou is obsessed with sniffing round Rockie's rear end. Fortunately, humans are not similarly obsessed although the habit could have made my teenage years more interesting.

29 July. Today I picked and tasted the first black blackberry of the year but it was tart so I will have to wait awhile before asking my wife to start preparing the crumble.

AUGUST

The first of August was the birthday of a great friend of ours, the late Sheila Hamilton, and she used to say that from this day onwards the nip of autumn could be sensed in the air. I stubbornly disagreed because I didn't want to accept that summer could be coming to an end.

***

Something that intrigues me on our walks round the lakes is the numerous animal tracks across the grass leading into shrubbery or down to the waterside; some are small and narrow, probably used by rabbits or weasels, others larger, wider ones are the paths of foxes, badgers and munjac.

Like humans with their roads and paths, mammals usually have preferred routes across the countryside instead of just wandering randomly through it. If all these trails could be plotted and charted the result would be a map as comprehensive and logical as a roadmap.

In former times, when our ancestors had a closer relationship with nature and the countryside, they were well acquainted with these mammalian routes and, like

Intuits with their many words for snow, had various terms for describing them.

In Suffolk "thorough-shutts" were the holes in hedges where rabbits passed through and in Lancashire a "hare gate" was an opening in a hedge made by hares; the Derbyshire word for the same feature was a "smout" and in Sussex a "smeuse" was a hedge-gap made by any small mammal. There were many words associated with deer; here in Northamptonshire the tracks made by them through shrubbery were "foylings" and, in the Cotswolds, "scorts" were the footprints of deer; also, the Northamptonshire term for rabbit footprints was "pricklings" but Cotswoldians called them "racks". The pastime of hunting also brought many words, for example, a "gallery" was a deer path and "foils" were their tracks; in Exmoor, if you followed animal tracks you were "spurring". Lastly, in Suffolk, "feetings" were the footprints of creatures in the snow.

I am indebted to the glossaries in Robert Macfarlane's scholarly and thought-provoking book *Landmarks* for the above words and definitions.

The Calf Path, a lengthy poem by American poet, Sam Walter Foss, describes the development of an animal track over the centuries from a trail made by a solitary calf to a road carrying "the traffic of a continent". These are some of the thirty-three verses that describe that progression:

One day through the primeval wood
A calf walked home as good calves should;

The trail was taken up next day,
By a lone dog that passed that way;

And then a wise bell-wether sheep
Pursued the trail o'er vale and steep.

The forest path became a lane,
That bent and turned and turned again.

The years passed on in swiftness fleet,
The road became a village street;

And this before men were aware,
A city's crowded thoroughfare.

And o'er his crooked journey went
The traffic of a continent.

A hundred thousand men were led,
By one calf near three centuries dead.

A beautifully conveyed transition which I sincerely hope doesn't happen to any of the animal tracks at Stanwick Lakes.

***

Along a narrow stretch of land between the path and the woods it was recently thick with oxeye daisies; these wilted and died, and soon a growth of felty leaves appeared, then their stalks grew to about two feet high covered in the soft furry foliage topped with the knob-heads of the flowers; finally, the flat-topped yellow daisy-like blooms of common fleabane decorated the path-side. It is remarkable that it grows in such profusion here yet isn't, as far as I know, present anywhere else at the lakes. The reason for this profusion is that common fleabane has roots that spread over the surface of the ground forming continuous coverage; in pedant parlance, this feature is called "stoloniferous".

Common fleabane is so named because it was formerly burnt in houses as an incense to drive away fleas. It was also used as a treatment to prevent dysentery and both usages are reflected in the plant's botanical name *pulicaria dysenterica*; *pulicaria* is derived from the Latin *pulex* meaning flea and the *dysenterica* is self-explanatory.

A rather more bizarre medicinal use of the flower is described in Miss E. S. Rohde's *Old English Herbal* which prescribes 'Fleabane bound to the forehead is a great helpe to cure one of the frensie.'

I don't know about you but I haven't suffered from any frenzy-like symptoms such as uncontrolled excitement or wild behaviour for some time, but if I do then I'll probably consider sellotaping some fleabane to my forehead.

***

The changing river-scape: The loop of the river that leaves the main Nene channel and rejoins it after passing through the nature reserve is gradually filling with rushes. Over recent months I have seen a few tufts of reed in the centre of the river-flow expand into a small island where coots and moorhens have nested. The reed growth on the adjacent bank is now spreading to join it and soon a channel will be blocked. On the river bed thick long fronds of reeds wave to and fro. This stretch was once popular with canoeists but is becoming overgrown and impassable.

During heavy rain a couple of months ago, when the river was in spate, a large part of a gnarled tree trunk with some short protruding branches floated downstream and became wedged against the brick supporting pier of the railway bridge; this tree trunk now has its own ecosystem. Leaved twigs have sprouted from it and many wildflowers including woody nightshade, bindweed, woundworts and the ever opportunist Himalayan balsam have managed to root, so now there is a lush growth and the trunk beneath is no longer visible. All this is also limiting the flow of water beneath the bridge.

I am waiting to see whether the rangers venture into the river, either in waders or in their boat, to dislodge the massive obstacle or whether it is just to be left to be absorbed into the riparian habitat.

Also, I see a small tail flicking vertically and repeatedly on the new trunk tree island; a wren has become a frequent visitor, probably looking for a boudoir where he can install one of his mistresses because male wrens are highly polygamous and service several breeding females. When I was at school, we had a headmaster called Mr. Wrenn but as far as we knew he only had one wife. The wren's scientific name is *troglodytes* which appropriately smacks of tribal pre-history because it means "cave dweller". Wrens get the name because of their habit of sneaking into crevices to hunt and roost. In folklore wrens were crowned "king of birds" which is very surprising considering they are one of our smallest birds. They received this title from one of Aesop's fables in which the wren challenged an eagle to see which could fly the highest; but the cunning wren sneaked on to the eagle's back and when the eagle wearied the wren flew off even higher, thereby proving cleverness wins over strength.

***

4 August. Last month when our friend, Trish, lost her Westie, Skye, I said I hoped she would soon get a replacement. I didn't have to wait long as today she excitedly introduced us to a new puppy, another Westie, called Logan. She was carrying it as it hasn't had all its injections and can't yet run around. Its level of cuteness is impossible to describe – right off the scale!

***

At this time of year I find it relaxing and enjoyable sitting in the garden watching the butterflies. Also, we have some seashell wind chimes hanging from a fence and their tinklings are an apt musical accompaniment to the butterflies' flutterings – very Zen. But my wife thinks I'm lazy and just loafing; she doesn't accept it as a valid excuse for not gardening when I tell her I'm busy observing the butterflies.

Some years ago, there was a glut of large and small white butterflies and when I went into the garden there must have been about thirty bobbing over the flower heads; they were also attracted to a buddleia which had rooted in the side of an old stone wall. I went and sat still and silently amongst the shrubbery and to my surprise several butterflies came and settled on me; they gently probed my skin with their proboscises and stretched their wings. I felt privileged and entrusted that they weren't threatened by my presence. Then they flapped away to find a tastier nectar. These were my thoughts:

You're welcome in my garden,
small white butterfly.
Your daintiness bestowed on me
as you pass by.

So haphazard and flappy,
so aimless is your flight.
Which blossom will you choose today?
Where will you alight?

Delicate, exquisite, frail,
the ballet that you dance,
no pattern to your progress,
all seemingly by chance.

Then up and away again,
so other gardens might be
blessed by your presence
the way you honoured me.

***

We are often greeted immediately on our arrival at Stanwick Lakes by pied wagtails which are attracted to the open areas around the car park and Visitor Centre. They are regularly seen in their black and white uniforms patrolling the Centre entrance path like commissionaires checking visitor admissions, but I don't think they would hold down a job at the Ritz because they fly off when someone comes.

Pied wagtails prefer open spaces, such as car parks, because they can easily see the insects they feed on and which they rapidly run after to catch. Ironically, their scientific family name is *motacilla,* so they were always destined to chase around places where motors were parked. I don't know who Cilla is unless Motacilla is the nickname of a Liverpudlian parking attendant. Maybe a ditty like this might be heard at a Liverpool car park;

Motacilla,
park my car,
over there
but not too far.
I need a quick
getaway.

I'm off to rob
a bank today.

12 August. Now that Caillou has recovered from his hip problem we had a longer ramble going over the river to walk along the Nene Way riverside path.

This route passes the Frontier Centre which sounds like something you would expect to be in the foothills of the Himalayas. Sometimes, when we pass the Centre it seems unoccupied and has a stalag-like eeriness about it; at other times, it is throbbing with activity and there are many course attendees and instructors there.

The Centre, operated by Rock UK, a Christian charity, covers 120 acres of beautiful Nene valley countryside and it can accommodate over two hundred residents. There is a wide range of activities, mainly water-based, making full use of the adjacent river and lakes. The charity was originally started in 1922 by some London Sunday school teachers who took a group of children, who had never been on holiday, to the seaside.

This is another of the amenities enabling the Nene valley to develop into a tourist area. It is largely being achieved through the government funded Nene Valley Nature Improvement Area. In recent years, I have seen the valley change from a series of flood-prone meadows, through which the river passes, to several nature-based leisure facilities the local population can enjoy.

I apologise for the plug but it shows how delighted and proud I am to have all this "on my doorstep".

Dave Rees and his Westie, Daisy, were with us this

morning and during the walk we had a moment of panic. There is a bridge over a side channel of the river and an old ford parallel to it. As it was a hot morning Dave took Daisy down to the ford for a drink; however, the Westie ventured into a strong current and, to our horror, was washed under the bridge and downstream. As usual in these situations, I knew I would have to take control and push either Dave or Ann into the river to save the dog but while I was bracing myself to take action it managed to swim into some reeds and halt its progress. Then it turned to swim back upstream but the flow was too strong; finally, it managed to catch a hold on some vegetation and, to our great relief, clamber through it and up the bank. The dog that emerged was no longer the snowy white Westie that had entered the water; whatever Dave had planned for the rest of the morning was now going to be partly taken up with a dog scrubbing session.

***

Stanwick Lakes has also been awarded the accolade of Northamptonshire's top family attraction; this means that the venue is very different, particularly at weekends and during the school holidays, to the peaceful nature reserve we early morning dog walkers experience. However, I am pleased about the family visitors because a recent survey by the National Trust has found that children today spend less than half the time outdoors that their parents did. Attractions such as the play area, assault course and adventure trail entice youngsters into the countryside and, hopefully on these visits, they will find an interest in the surroundings.

When we arrive early on Monday mornings the rangers and volunteers are busy litter picking, equipment checking etc. ready for the hordes to return. But what amazes me, is the amount of children's clothing left behind which often seems enough to open a branch of Mothercare. There are small trainers, T-shirts, toddlers' fleece sweaters, socks – lots of little socks – and babies' dummies. I can't understand how parents can bring little Tyrone to the Lakes fully clothed and take him home semi-naked without realising it.

14 August. In the newspaper today there is an article on, and photograph of, our new leader, Theresa May, on a walking holiday in Switzerland with her husband, Phil. I thought, regardless of political affiliations, she was a like-minded, nature-loving person who shared my passion for walking in the countryside. Also, she was enjoying a simple holiday, like the ones we have, and not swanning about on an oligarch's super-yacht or loafing, cocktail in hand, on some billionaire's private beach. (But, to be honest, I wouldn't mind having a chance of either of these).

Maybe, when she has settled into her new job and sorted out this Europe business, I will invite her to Stanwick Lakes for a walk with me and Caillou although I can't imagine her carrying a dog-poo bag; she'd probably hand it to Phil or one of the bodyguards tagging along behind.

17 August. Dave and I were looking over the bridge handrail at the new tree trunk island – no, not Dave Rees, who walked round the Nene Way with us a few days ago, but another Dave, Dave Goodier. Anyway, we were looking at the burgeoning vegetation on the tree trunk when Dave commented on a bright orange flower we hadn't noticed before. There are not many wildflowers of that colour in this country so I easily tracked it down. It is orange balsam, a relative of the infamous Himalayan balsam but, whereas the latter is from the Indian sub-continent, the former is a native of North America.

Orange balsam was introduced into this country in the nineteenth century; I don't need to tell you what I think about the Victorians. However, orange balsam is not so invasive as its Asian cousin because it does not grow in dense stands that stifle other vegetation. The small orange flowers are like bonnets, even like policemen's helmets, and in North America, the flower has a couple of unusual names; firstly, "touch-me not" because when the ripe seed capsules are touched, they explode sending the seeds metres away; the seeds also float down rivers before finding somewhere to sow, making it an almost exclusively riparian plant. (In this country, we also have a balsam called "touch-me-not" but this one has a yellow flower.) The other name is "jewelweed" because, when the leaves are underwater, they have a pearly silver sheen.

As with many plants, orange balsam once had a medicinal use, in this case as a cure for skin complaints; the crushed leaves were rubbed on the affected part of the body. It can even be used as a treatment for athlete's foot if you could tolerate a wodge of it between your toes.

***

We haven't had much rain for some time so the lake water levels are dropping and new mud-flat islands are surfacing. Birds, mainly gulls, soon occupy the new territory; actually, they don't even wait for the islands to appear as, prior to that, they paddle around ankle deep in the shallows.

Whilst looking at the newly found lands on Tern Island Lake, I notice a change on Oak Island, imaginatively named because it is dominated by a massive oak tree. Where the foliage used to be all a lush green, a section of it is now turning brown. I was concerned the tree was becoming diseased but through my binoculars I could see that one of the major branches had partially snapped off and was hanging down, consequently the leaves on it were dying. When I spoke to Dave the ranger he told me the collapse had occurred about two months ago.

Oak Island is near the location where the remains of a Roman villa were discovered during pre-quarrying archaeological exploration from 1984 to 1992. The villa was believed to have been inhabited for over two hundred years and was the central building of a farm estate that provided food for the surrounding communities. The most significant discovery was an ornate mosaic floor which was restored, at a cost of over ten thousand pounds, by Northamptonshire County Council. It was money well spent because it is now on display at the Visitor Centre and is worth seeing.

The villa probably also owes its location to the proximity of the river which could be used for transport and as a thoroughfare.

I try to picture the normal everyday lives of the wealthy Romans as they wandered around their luxurious home in togas, but my imagination refuses to move on from visions of bacchanalia.

***

A rant of elderly curmudgeonliness: There has been a mini-heatwave and in the Stanwick Lakes barbeque area and the gardens surrounding our home this has caused an epidemic of SBM (Seasonal Barbeque Mania). This involves the ritual immolation of animal flesh to produce charcoal and is an imprudent process largely carried out by men, with a can of warm lager in hand, on a device over which they have little thermal control. The result is quoits of burnt processed animal gristle wedged between two lumps of similar sized spongy bread substitute. No one can ever persuade me it should come in the same category as cooking.

I did buy a barbeque once so I could be trendy and "with-it"; first the smoke from the charcoal gave me a coughing fit then I spent some time, with eyes running, turning over some chicken pieces on the grill. After, what seemed like a long time, my wife and I studied the results of my cooking and decided we could risk food poisoning by eating something that we were uncertain was properly cooked; so, we took it indoors and finished the process in the oven. Since then the barbeque has stood collecting dust in the garage accompanied by a nearly full bag of charcoal.

However, we have been invited to some of these outdoor social gatherings and, don't get me wrong, we have enjoyed the occasion and being in the convivial company of friends; (so please don't stop inviting us.) it's just the food I haven't particularly enjoyed.

Also, I have a theory that the reason heatwaves don't last long in this country is because the smoky blue haze rising from multiple barbeques into the stratosphere, or whatever, eventually filters the heat from the sun's rays. My other belief is that the so-called dog days of summer should be renamed the hot dog days.

I don't know whether there is a patron saint of barbeques but, if there isn't, I would like to nominate Joan of Arc because she had the necessary experience of uncontrolled burning.

***

Due to the recent lack of rain, the grass is turning a pale beige and, because of the dryness, the leaves on some trees are prematurely withering to autumn brown.

However, the dry hot weather has brought an early bonus to the farmer who has the right to harvest the hay at Stanwick Lakes as all open grass areas have been cut and, in places, round bales await collection. So, the land recently covered in high vegetation, is now "lawned" limiting the places where species can conceal themselves and today, the twenty-fourth, we saw a roe deer, the first one I have seen at the Lakes, as it raced across the open ground into the woods.

Since identifying orange balsam a week ago, I am now finding it flowering regularly beside lakes.

28 August. Today is a significant day in the history of this country – my seventy-fifth birthday! I had a suspicion my family were planning to buy me a voucher for one of those "experiences" such as bungee jumping, sky diving or swimming with sharks but fortunately it didn't materialise as I am not in need of those type of thrills at the moment. Instead I plumped for a leisurely family Sunday lunch at the Duke of Wellington pub in Stanwick. When I heard my son and daughter arranging a taxi there and back I knew they weren't intending to drink only Perrier.

After the meal, the waitress brought my birthday cake which my granddaughter, Emma, had made. It had a few candles on it but not one for every year of my life because it was feared that could cause the Stanwick villagers to think there was a torchlight procession.

So, I was born in 1941 in the thick of World War Two; my father was away in the Navy, but I prefer to believe he was home on leave nine months earlier. My mother called me her "little war effort".

The most interesting birthday card I received was from Dave, my walking pal, and his wife Maureen; this card contained a list of facts about the year I was born.

In 1941 aerosol fly sprays and Vecro were invented and Delia Smith, Neil Diamond and Bob Dylan were also born; I always thought they looked a lot older than me. In those pre-rap days, the most popular song was "Bewitched, Bothered and Bewildered" which ironically is precisely how I often feel now. The average wage in 1941 was £4.97 a week, now it is £510; the price of a bottle of whisky was £0.88 – the price had soared due to black market racketeering – now it is £14.80, and a pint of beer has gone up from £0.04 to around £3.50. Wages have multiplied by 103, whisky amazingly by only 17 and beer by 88 which mean that at least now we are all "booze richer".

 # SEPTEMBER

143

September the first is the beginning of meteorological autumn; blimey, that summer didn't seem to last long!

September derives from the Latin *septum,* meaning seventh, because it was originally the seventh month of the old ten-month Roman calendar year. This changed in 153 BC when the Roman bosses decided they needed a couple more months at the beginning of the year, so January and February were introduced demoting September to ninth place. They no doubt needed these two extra months to recover from the New Year's Eve's bacchanals and still return to work sober on the first of March as usual.

When Theresa May accepts my invitation to come for a walk at Stanwick Lakes, I intend to suggest to her that we also should have an extra "holiday" month in the year; I'm sure it would increase her popularity and we could even name the month after her although, to avoid confusion, we would have to think of something other than May.

In the USA, September is "Better Breakfast Month" and "National Childhood Obesity Awareness Month". It occurs to me that if they had less of the former there would be less need for the latter.

This year nature has really taken advantage of the extremely favourable weather conditions and all the vegetation has grown to record proportions, everything being rich, green and lush. Trees and shrubs are taller, leafier and generally more prolific than recent years making the woods into impenetrable jungles of Amazonian density. Brambles have sent their long gangly shoots out to dangle like waving thorny wands into open spaces. Reeds and rushes fill the river and are encroaching further into the water from the lake fringes; some of the smaller lakes are less visible from the paths having become screened by high foliage, notably willow shoots.

It is not only the flora which is profuse as the birds have also bred well particularly the water birds; unlike previous years, they have not had their early nest building attempts washed away by late flooding.

All this makes Stanwick Lakes very beautiful but presents a nature management challenge to the rangers. When quarrying finished in 2004 and the area first became a nature reserve and leisure amenity, it was mainly open wetland; since then sections of it have become more of a woodland habitat. Therefore, one of the issues is that tall trees have started to surround the lakes obstructing the flight paths of wildfowl dissuading them from sweeping down on to the water: so the range of species visiting the lakes also changes. That's the dilemma: do you leave nature to take its own course or do you try to manage it to maintain a certain habitat? Probably in this case it would mainly have to be the latter because Stanwick Lakes has been awarded the status of a Site of Special Scientific Interest (SSSI) which requires the area to be protected through active management to conserve the flora and fauna.

***

I commented back in May that it was a time of whiteness, particularly with regards to the hawthorn blossom. Now it has become its time of redness, as the hawthorns are exceptionally heavily laden with their berries. Also, many other shrubs are adorned with berries: rose hips on the dog roses: reddish pink grape-like clusters on the guelder-roses: similar black ones on the alder buckthorn: sloes will soon be ready for harvesting on the blackthorn; in the past, my wife has made sloe gin from the fruits of this tree but I think that's a sacrilegious waste of neat gin.

Although the blackberry brambles have lots of fruit, this year the berries are of poor quality and few of them are suitable for my beloved apple and blackberry crumble – preferably doused in full cream. The berries are plentiful but small and even those that have blackened haven't sweetened. However, every year there is a particular stretch of bramble hedge, at the far end of the small lake near the Visitor Centre, which always has the best yield. This year, when we went to gather our dessert ingredients, the grass along the bottom of the hedge was flattened and someone had stolen all the lower fruit; of course, I blamed it on mammals of the human variety but others are known to feast on the lower berries. In his richly bucolic and poetic book *Meadowland,* John Lewis Stempel comments that he saw a young fox standing on its hind legs plucking a blackberry from a bush. I wonder what his mum uses for crumble.

4 September. I was milling around with other athletes this morning as there was a 5 km, 10 km and half marathon run at the Lakes. I hadn't entered any of these but had come to cheer on two friends, Ali Blair and her sister Jo, who were participating. The reason I didn't enter the event was because I was worried about falling foul of the Doping Agency as I have been known to take performance enhancing alcohol. I used to regularly go out for a jog down the fields but now it would more likely be for a jug down the pub.

***

Helios, the God of Sun recently answered my prayers for some summer weather and he also lends his name to plant sun worshippers. These flowers that turn their heads towards him in reverence are called heliotropic and the most famous acolyte is the sunflower. But amongst the thick tall growth is another, rather unremarkable and unappealing, flower that has the same habit, and it has the industrial name of Weld. This tall plant – it grows to about five feet – has long spear-like yellowy green clusters of flowers up its ribbed stems which twist and contort towards the sun even when it is cloudy. Plants that have flowers like those of Weld which are radially symmetrical have the terrifically sci-fi name of zygomophic; this word can be usefully added to one's vocabulary or casually dropped into conversations; it will even score an impressive, game winning, thirty-four points at Scrabble regardless of additional points gained through landing on pink or blue bonus squares. Anyway, Weld was also used commercially to produce a lemony yellow dye, luteolin, and because of that, and the plant's long pointed shape, it is also called dyer's rocket.

***

In April I commented that the poet John Clare probably quoted Shakespeare and now I can confirm that he did. For my birthday, my daughter Melanie, bought me a book of John Clare's autobiographical writings and in it he mentions that, in his teenage years, he read Shakespeare and Milton.

I knew a bit about John Clare – that he was born in Northamptonshire, came from peasant stock and ended his life in a lunatic asylum – but I felt I would like to know more about him. While reading the book, *John Clare, By Himself,* I have formed a high opinion of him. Very sadly, as his reputation was rising and he was becoming ranked alongside other major poets such as Byron and Shelley, he became beset by mental illness and spent the last twenty years of his life in the lunatic asylum in Northampton; this caused his standing to wane at the time and it seems that, due to his insanity, he was probably prevented from taking his rightful position in the poets' hierarchy.

What strikes me about his work is that he writes as though he is a natural medium through which nature expresses itself poetically. He came from humble beginnings, was poorly educated, although self-taught, and worked mainly as a labourer on the land in his early years. But this closeness to nature triggered a creative spark and, largely distanced from the influence of other writers, he had an innate urge to record his life in the countryside.

I recommend his works to anyone who enjoys poetry as it describes our land and countryside and the poet's life in it. I intend to try and get a John Clare T-shirt!

Anyway, that's enough of my arty-farty pontificating; I must get back down to earth and, while there, what better subject to write about than moles which are exceptionally active right now. Moles live in an underground tunnel system which they dig themselves, and it is an ongoing project as the earthworks are extended in the moles' search for food; this is mainly earthworms which the moles paralyse with a toxin in their saliva. They then cleverly bite off the front end of the worms — which amazingly remain alive — providing the moles with a larder of fresh food for the winter months.

There are several reasons why moles are particularly active now: firstly, the young have left their mothers and are working on a tunnel system of their own: secondly, after the mating season moles separate from their partners and dig their own private subway: thirdly, they are furiously foraging underground to build up their winter earthworm larder.

What better way to finish this than a verse from John Clare's love poem, *Meet Me in the Green Glen.*

Meet me by the sweetbriar,
By the molehill swelling there;
When the west glows like a fire
God's crimson bed is there.
Meet me in the green glen.

10 September. There was a triathlon at the Lakes today and scores of unnaturally healthy and toned humans were gathering waiting for the event to start. When I presented myself to the organisers they claimed they had not received my application so I would not be allowed to compete. Or, maybe, on seeing my two walking sticks, they concluded my attempts at participation were less than serious so they had crossed out my name.

We watched the start of the first event, the swimming, as the competitors, wearing orange caps (like my wife's swimming one but without the pretty little plastic flowers) plunged, wetsuit-clad into the lake then splashed and frantically crawl-swam like a pod of seals being panicked by pursuing killer whales.

I am considering organising a similar event for elderly dog walkers, possibly called a Hoblathon, but

I haven't yet worked out a points system or how it can be made competitive. Here are some suggestions for possible events: Activity 1: hobbling along at full speed with the spine curved over slightly to one side: Activity 2: ineffectively attempting to sidestep fast moving cyclists and joggers: Activity 3: trying to remember why you came down to the Lakes in the first place.

**

A flash of white in the willows by the river and another on the opposite bank, then, spooked by our approach, two great spotted woodpeckers flee-fly off and are lost to us in the woods.

There have been quite a few sightings of less frequently sighted birds at the Lakes recently; these are recorded by the rangers on a chalkboard near their cabin and include dunlins, ruffs, common sandpipers and turnstones. Also, bird expert Bob Webster, told me that there has been a shag at the Lakes. Of course, I haven't seen any of these; if I intend to have any success as a serious birdwatcher I would need to become a sort of "second-hand" twitcher and not only tick off the birds I have seen in my bird book but also those that other people have told me they have seen.

However, I have noticed that the lapwings have returned to regain possession of the islands from which they were ousted by black-headed gulls some months ago. Where have they been? Lapwings migrate to the UK from the continent in the winter to avoid the cold weather and find milder conditions, then they return when things improve – very sensible!

13 September. I was going to write that signs of autumn are making more frequent appearances with a few leaves turning yellow and brown and others already fluttering daintily to the ground; flocks of swallows are swooping around in the sky training their youngsters for the long-haul flight south; the swifts have already gone. Then, overnight summer returns tropically and the temperature passes thirty-two degrees, the hottest September day for fifty-seven years, putting nature's autumn plan temporarily on hold.

When we last had this level of September heat in 1959, Soviet satellite Lunik 2 became the first man-made object to land on the moon, crashing down on to the Sea of Tranquillity which I believe had to be renamed the Sea of Terrific Noise and Scrap Metal.

The brief Indian summer brought another record; it was the first time since 1929 that September temperatures had exceeded thirty degrees on three consecutive days. But, of course, it couldn't go on, and on the fourth day temperatures plummeted, there was torrential rain and violent thunderstorms.

On the last day of the heat there were signs presaging change; a heavy mist was draped across the valley blending the greys of the lake with the woodland background and the sky: no delineation at all; the lake island birds stood ghostly and gaunt, not tempted by thoughts of flight up into the murk.

17 September. I have been waiting for the hazel nuts to be ready for me to gather but when I went to look for them they'd been nicked; squirrels had taken them for their winter larder. I know they are guilty because they couldn't resist snacking during harvesting and had left tell-tale shells on the ground with teeth-mark surrounded incisions. I shoulder-shrug; they doubtless have greater need for them than I, who would just scoff a few with a preprandial snifter.

I have encountered several references to the use of hazel wood recently; for example, in a book by Kate Mosse she mentions a man who has a hazel walking stick and in the fascinating and extremely interesting television documentary, *Britain's Pompeii*, it describes how hazel rods were used in the construction of Bronze Age roundhouses, particularly for the roof rafters.

Many years ago, hazel poles were favoured by pilgrims to ease the rigours of their long journeys; similarly, the poles were the preferred wood for shepherds' crooks as well as walking sticks. Also, our ancestors used the forked twigs for water divining and the leaves as cattle fodder. The actual nuts were ground into flour to make bread: the trees were, and still are, coppiced to produce long new twigs for hurdles, fence wattles and basketry so not much of the tree was wasted. The nuts are often called "filberts" after Saint Philbert's day, the twentieth of August, when the nuts are supposed to start ripening. Obviously, the squirrels have this date clearly marked in their diaries!

***

There is a path at the north end of Stanwick Lakes which is rarely walked because it is a grass, unpaved track passing through fields where a farmer often keeps stock. Also, the path isn't marked in the free map available at the Visitor Centre and it isn't signposted – perhaps they don't want us to walk it! But it is shown as a bridleway on the Ordnance Survey map (Explorer 224).

The path is called the Hog Dyke after the brook which runs alongside part of it; this brook carries watershed from the Raunds area into the River Nene.

It is about four miles as a circular walk starting and finishing at the Stanwick Lakes car park so it is really a bit too far for my arthritic legs. I have attempted it twice, the first time anticlockwise joining the Hog Dyke near the A45 underpass; the route was initially alongside a fence then headed across a field but I couldn't work out the direction it took; I should have taken a map and compass so I could have set the bearing. After wandering about and failing to find the point where the path joined the old railway track I gave up and retraced my steps.

On my second attempt, I tried it in a clockwise direction and actually found the gate that led to the Hog Dyke but the path was very muddy so I didn't proceed any further.

I feel defeated and deflated at these failures but, on a day when my joint pain has eased a bit, I hope to have another attempt.

However, the reason I am recommending this walk is

because the route runs alongside a field which contains the remains of the deserted medieval village of Mallows Cotton which is of such significance that it is scheduled under the Ancient Monuments and Archaeological Areas Act of 1979. Like the similar village of West Cotton, one kilometre to the south, it was found to have comprised houses, gardens, streets, a manor house and a church. It originated in the twelfth century and was known to have been abandoned by the eighteenth. It was a community devoted to agriculture and its desertion is attributed to economic agricultural decline and probably factors such as the Black Death epidemic.

The word "Cotton" appears regularly in British place names and it derives from the Old English word "cotum" meaning cottages or dwellings.

For anyone interested in walking past the Mallows Cotton remains there is another alternative route; Janice Morris, the wife of an acquaintance of mine, Phil Morris, has written a guide to a six-mile circular ramble called the Mallows Cotton Walk which starts in the square at Ringstead (www.ringsteadpc.org.uk).

***

I have reluctantly missed several mornings at the Lakes due to a chesty cough cold. I tried all recommended cures including Lemsips, Benylin, Strepsils, Covonia vapour drops and even a little white Vick dildo thing I used to penetrate my nostrils. Finally, the doctor prescribed antibiotics and I am slowly recovering. Colds have a life to lead and are determined to extract the full measure, from birth through a sneeze to demise through surrender to clear headedness, and no medicines seem capable of shortening that life.

20 September. I am off to Spain for nearly three weeks on Thursday so I am afraid the dog walkers of Stanwick Lakes will be deprived of my witty banter in the mornings. But they shouldn't become too downhearted because I am sure I will have lots of tales to amuse them with when I come back.

21 September. One last stroll round the Lakes before I leave: a quiet, still, brisk, clear morning, harbinger of autumn: a robin is perched at the end of the roof ridge on the rangers' cabin beautifully trilling his broadcast through the crisp morning air: a forked dead tree branch sticks into the skyline above the woodland greenery; a solitary sentinel crow sits silhouetted on top – just looking round.

OCTOBER

The Spanish Digression: please excuse me while I deviate from the subject of Stanwick Lakes and include some snippets from my Spain notebook.

Would you believe it? The house we rented was owned by yet another Dave.

***

On our previous trips to Spain we had flown, but this time I thought it would be a good idea to try and travel there on buses; however, when I found out that the French and Spanish wouldn't accept our senior citizen bus passes, I abandoned that plan. I believe it should be a central plank of our negotiations over Brexit that UK retirees have free travel on public transport in Europe or we refuse to buy their cars, wine and cheese – except maybe at discount pensioner prices; something else for me to suggest to Theresa when I meet her at the Lakes.

Anyway, our son, Clive, offered to drive us to Spain so we could take our dogs, Caillou and Rockie.

***

On the second night of our journey south, we stayed at a hotel opposite the bullring in the Rioja region town of Alfaro; there wasn't any bullfighting scheduled to take place during our stay or I would have definitely have entered the *corrida* for arthritic amateur matadors. Typically for Spain, the hotel restaurant didn't open until eight thirty and dogs were not allowed entry so, wishing to eat earlier, we sauntered into the town centre in search of food.

Cafes, bars and restaurants lined the narrow streets and surrounded the square in front of the main church. The pavement tables were packed with people of all ages – the elderly, teenagers and young families all happily enjoying their Friday night out and socially interacting while they ate and drank; young children raced around playing together. It was a sort of communal gathering we seldom experience in the UK where we don't have the warm balmy evenings and the weather confines us indoors in small social groups.

Finally, we found a bar where the owner allowed us to enter with our dogs and we had a tapas meal washed down with a bottle of the recommended Rioja.

Replete, as we dawdled back to our hotel, fascinated by the crowds thronging around, two tall, raven-haired, heavily made up Good Time Girls – *las damas de la noche* – at least I thought they were female, came sashaying down the street in vicious impossibly high heels and indecently short figure-hugging dresses. I inspected them furtively out the corner of my eye knowing that at the least noticeable hint of a gawp I would receive a sharp elbow dig in the ribs from Ann.

'Did you see those women?' she asked.

I looked bemused. 'No. Where? What women?' I said innocently.

She glared at me disbelievingly. I pulled a false sardonic smile. I'd got away with it.

***

Our rented house was in the vast urbanisation of Villamartin so, to exercise Caillou, we had to walk the streets; consequently, we began to suffer from countryside deprivation. To remedy this, we drove to the Parc Natural de la Mata-Torrevieja. This nature reserve is centred round two large lakes each many times larger than any of those at Stanwick; the bigger one, the Salinas de Torrevieja, is 1400 hectares and the other one is 700 hectares. To get this into perspective the entire area of the Stanwick Lakes reserve is just over 300 hectares so it would fit into the larger Salinas over four and a half times.

As the name Salinas implies these are salt lakes and, with the surrounding salt marshes, are wetlands of international importance; they are also zones for the special protection of birds (ZEPA). However, this is not a natural environment that has beauty anything like that of the lush, rich, verdant and varied English countryside; it is parched and arid with a few clusters of trees. It occurs to me that if you take the English countryside, mathematically add the Sahara desert and divide by two the answer's Spain.

Our walk was of about two hours' duration mostly

in inescapable heat of thirty degrees. The small areas of woodland provided welcome heavenly coolth. These oases are Aleppo pines, eucalyptus and kermes oak (their acorns litter the floor beneath).

There are several bird hides around the lake and from these the most spectacular sight is the flamingos which often gather in flocks of two thousand. I looked forward to seeing the bird experts at Stanwick so I could boast I had seen flamingos last week; disappointingly, they are not in my bird book so I can't even tick them off to add them to my twitching score. A grey heron also stalked the lake fringes and an avocet worked the shallows. Later, a black and yellow butterfly flitted by the path; it was a type of swallowtail, species rare in Britain. By the time we had finished our walk, we had drank several bottles of water and probably sweat off a couple of pounds in weight.

Areas of Stanwick Lakes are used for cattle grazing and at this Parc Natural the local agriculturalists also use part of the land. However, here it is used as vineyards to grow the wine producing Moscatel and Merseguera grapes which I think is a much better use of land than for sheep and cows. As England is now becoming more of a wine producing nation, I intend to suggest to the management at Stanwick Lakes that part of the meadows there become a vineyard. This wine could then be distributed to the regular walkers at Christmas, New Year, Easter, Spring and Summer Bank holidays, Halloween and Bonfire Night, and also at the, soon to be announced, two week public Brexit celebration holiday next June – if Theresa agrees with my proposal.

***

On this holiday we were kindly lent a Mercedes Smart car to run around in. This is like a normal car but with the back half lopped off; it is rather like driving around in a reduced height telephone booth.

On our first drive, we managed to get to a *Mercadona* supermarket for our first "big shop". Unfortunately, afterwards we failed to find a way to open the boot. I tried all combinations of key zaps and we ran our fingers under every rimmed edge searching for the elusive catch but couldn't find the cursed thing. The situation was made worse because it was impossible to get to the boot from inside the car because it was partitioned off. So Ann sat on the passenger seat and I piled the numerous shopping bags on top of her and around her legs. When I had finished, all that was visible of Ann were two arms sticking out. On the way home, I asked if she was OK and all I heard was a muffled grunt which I prayed wasn't a death rattle. The journey was made worse because initially I failed to find the automatic gear. The car has four gear stick positions – automatic, first, neutral and reverse – but I could only shift it into "first" so we slowly pootled along with the engine screeching like a banshee. However, on my second lay-by stop to play with the gear lever I got it into "automatic" (the secret was to press a little button beneath the gear stick knob) and then we cruised home at an acceptable level of decibels.

My son showed me later that the boot release button

doesn't open the actual boot but the rear window; this is lifted and the rest of the boot is bottom hinged and can be lowered by releasing a catch either side.

For decades we have been having cars with boots that satisfactorily opened with top-hinged doors so what sadistic perverted car designer came up with that complicated barmy idea? I can imagine them in their design studio saying, 've hav vays ov vrustating der stupid Englanders, ya?' then all looking at the design concept and roaring with laughter.

OK, so we won't buy your cars after Brexit. Ya?

***

A clowder of feral cats had made its headquarters in the grounds of an unoccupied villa opposite the house we were renting and every afternoon, while I sat reading on the veranda, a lady arrived and shoved some food under the gate. The cats then rapidly appeared from all directions for a feast. Waiting in the surrounding trees were some collared doves and, when the cats had finished eating, they descended to peck at the leftovers; next some house sparrows arrived and hopped around the doves before finally feasting on the leftover leftovers – a veritable pecking order.

3 October. This afternoon we drove to a resort called Lo Pagan where there is a coastal lagoon and nature reserve, the Parque Regional de las Salinas y Arenales de San Pedro. (I love the lengthy names the Spanish give to their amenities and when I get back to Stanwick Lakes I intend to start a campaign to have it renamed "The Regional Nature Reserve of Lakes and Meadows of Stanwick and Ringstead".)

This sulphurous, farty, rotten egg smelling lake is where people coat their bodies in the obnoxious dark grey slime and let it dry in the belief it can cure many ailments. I had to a have a go! So, I slipped into my budgie smugglers, waded into the lake, scooped up handfuls of the mud and smeared it on the parts of my body which I felt needed reviving; I haven't noticed any improvements yet but it is the most fun I have had playing with mud since I was seven years old.

A pair of flamingos was in the water next to the pedestrian causeway; they seemed tame and ignored the people passing close by; they continued their vocation of curving their elegant necks down, dipping their heads into the water and ploughing forward with their stubby beaks to filter food from the mud.

***

Here are some interesting facts I learnt in Spain. They have trouble with the word "whisky" and spell it "guisqui" but no problem with "gin and tonic" which is "gin-tonic". Zaragoza was originally named Caesar Augusta two thousand years ago in honour of the, then ruling, Roman emperor and its present name has evolved from that over the centuries.

***

12 October. On our first morning back at Stanwick Lakes, Dave was waiting for us on the old railway bridge near the bird hide. I asked him if he had seen anything interesting while we were away but he said there hadn't been any exceptional sightings.

He is right; this is often a quiet time of the year in the countryside. The summer bird visitors have left but the winter migrants are still to arrive so, for a few weeks, the residents have the place to themselves which must delight the avian Brexiteers.

Also, I was surprised how little the trees had changed to their autumn tints and were still holding their verdure. However, most of the wildflowers have wilted away except the white dead-nettles which are making a comeback and blooming again. It is rather sad when the beautiful vivid and varied summer colours of the flowers depart the countryside leaving a panorama of greens.

***

Whilst reading John Clare's poems I have found a word he uses and which I like; it is "soodle" and it means to linger, saunter or dawdle whilst taking in your surroundings. I thought, *that's what I like to do*.

Something that surprises me is that Northants doesn't capitalise more on its connection with Clare as he is generally acknowledged to be England's greatest nature poet. He was born on the thirteenth of July 1793 so I suggest we declare that date "John Clare Day" and all go down the pub and recite his poetry – beards and sandals obligatory.

Also, in these days of concern about mental health the fact that, when Clare was in an asylum, he still managed to compose exceptional verse is an example that, even in the darkest of mental states, creative fulfilment is still achievable; I am sure that today, with support, it would have helped to coax him towards recovery.

I find that Clare's poems, like all poetry, are best appreciated if they are read slowly and with concentration particularly if read aloud, although, if my family caught me doing that whilst alone I, too, would probably be committed to an asylum.

14 October. On our walk this morning we met Ian Wrisdale and his wife. Ian was carrying a ladder and was going to evict a squirrel that had made its winter quarters in a stock dove nest box. Stock doves have a second brood in October, the first being in March, so it is important that they are not disturbed at this time. Ian told us that he had recorded thirteen fledglings in the boxes recently. Stock doves are like wood pigeons but are slightly smaller and don't have the white wing bars, and they are the only members of the pigeon family that use nest boxes.

Ian is a licensed bird ringer and organises the very interesting and informative ringing sessions at Stanwick Lakes – try and go along to one if you can. Bird ringing is carried out under the auspices of the British Trust for

Ornithology and there are three groups operating in Northamptonshire.

Also, Ian monitors and records the activity in the numerous bird boxes around the Lakes providing invaluable information about fluctuations in the bird population.

***

In a certain location, there is a large walnut tree and the ground beneath it is dotted with hundreds of nuts – or it was until I arrived with my plastic bag, now the nuts are in our kitchen where each afternoon we have a cracking session.

I then lightly roast the kernels until they are dry and crunchy but not browned then we snack on them whilst having our pre-dinner aperitif. I also use them to make a delicious walnut loaf which I have a slice of, generously layered with butter, with my afternoon cuppa.

I suppose you think Bob's just gorging himself again but, in this case, I have some justification for my nut consumption. Walnuts are considered to be the healthiest of nuts and reduce high cholesterol as well as the risk of both prostate and breast cancer; furthermore, they contain an amino acid, which brings benefit to those with heart disease, and neuro-protective compounds which help brain health and reasoning, Finally, a quarter of a cup of walnuts provides the daily recommended amount of omega three fats.

So, if you catch me with a glass in one hand and a pile of walnuts in the other, you can now be assured I am only working on my health and fitness.

***

A few widgeon have arrived but not yet the massed flocks; apparently, the weather in their summer quarters is still mild so their migration urge has not been triggered; furthermore, their arrival will now be more delayed because the wind has swung round to a strong south westerly causing a headwind for birds migrating from the north east; they'll no doubt have a short stopover on their way until wind directions are more favourable.

If I was a widgeon-husband flying south for the winter, instead of heading for grey and miserable England, I would try and persuade my widgeon-wife to press on to Marbella.

24 October. This morning we crossed the Staunch bridge and walked along the path by the river. This is part of the 110-mile-long waymarked Nene Way long distance path which starts at Badby in the south west corner of the county and finishes at Sutton Bridge in Lincolnshire. About twenty-five years ago, before arthritis restricted my walking capabilities, Ann and I walked the section to Peterborough in several stages with the Wellingborough Ramblers. Sadly, not many people seem to walk the Nene Way nowadays which is regrettable because it is an attractive, mainly riverside route, passing through many pretty villages.

When we reached the locks, we had an interesting encounter. A man was at the electric control panel which operates the lock gates. He was elderly with a characterful ruddy face and long white, curly haired sideburns under a Budweiser baseball cap. I asked him if he was travelling by narrow boat; he pointed into the lock and his barge was deep in the bottom. It was an old, battered vessel with various items stacked on top and, on hearing my voice, a dog barked from inside it. I asked him if he was travelling far.

'A place near Downham Market,' he replied.

'Have you had a narrow boat for long?'

'I've been on 'em nearly all my life, since I was fifteen.'

He then told us his parents had been publicans and when he finished school, his mother told him there was a job available on the barges so he went for an interview. All the interviewer was interested in was if he had a bike and could he lift it above his head. He had a bike which he had assembled from parts he had found, scrounged or been given; also, he could lift it above his head so he got the job. He was required to lift the bike on to canal paths, river banks and over various obstacles and, carrying a windlass, cycle to the next lock and begin raising or lowering the gates for the boat's arrival. He was paid three pounds a week plus board and lodging on the barge. He went, with his master, on three-day trips delivering wheat to granaries. I thought it was a pity that form of transport couldn't be used more nowadays to reduce the number of lorries on the roads.

He next told us that for several years he had been a

long-distance lorry driver delivering cargoes to Russia, Asia and Africa but now he had returned to his former life and lived fulltime on his beloved barge.

I said he must have had an interesting and eventful life and he should write it all down.

'Only one problem with that,' he said, 'I can't read or write.'

As we left he told me his name was Mick, I shook his hand, thanked him for taking time to chat to us and wished him all the best on his travels.

'I'll carry on barging till I reach the box,' he said.

'Box?' I queried.

'Yes, my coffin, that's what's waiting for me at the end of my travels and I'll carry on happily barging till I reach it.'

As we walked away I thought about him; he must be a determined and resourceful person to have led that life, and travelled great distances as a lorry driver, while having to overcome the issues presented by his illiteracy.

***

Autumn has really arrived and many leaves changed colour within a week. Also, the sun is sinking in the sky and early on clear breezy mornings its orangey rays slant sideways through the trees illuminating the golden leaves and streaking the paths with shimmering bands of brightness.

***

The recent mild and wet autumn weather has caused fungi to flourish; clusters of common puffballs have appeared amongst the grass and the phallic, and appropriately named Shaggy Ink Caps, *amanita phalloides* (the latter means phallus shaped), are thrusting upwards.

However, experts are warning that the conditions are also encouraging the deadly poisonous Death Cap to grow abundantly. As little as half of one of these contains enough toxins to kill a person, and as recently as 2006, a family of three in Poland was poisoned; one died and the other two had to have liver transplants; in Roman times, the emperor Claudius was assassinated by being fed a meal of Death Caps concealed as his favoured Caesar's mushrooms.

So, mushroom foragers should beware, because Death Caps are not dissimilar to many edible field mushrooms except that they grow mainly under broad leaf trees, whereas field mushrooms are more common in open areas such as meadows and pastures.

Some years ago, when we lived in France, one morning we went mushrooming with Colette, a French friend. Amongst the mushrooms we gathered was a large flat one which we weren't sure was edible.

In France, because there are many fungi foragers, pharmacists provide a service whereby they identify any specimens brought to them and advise whether they can be eaten; they even provide suggestions regarding how they are best cooked.

So, we took our mushroom to the pharmacist in

Mirambeau and the lady told us it was edible but not worth bothering with because, when cooked, it would liquefy into an unpleasant mush. I therefore learnt two things from the pharmacy visit; firstly, not to bother to pick those particular mushrooms and secondly, I learnt that the French word for "mush" was *bouillie* but I haven't had the occasion to need it since.

NOVEMBER

November gets its name from *Novem* the Latin for "nine" because it was originally the ninth month before the Romans slipped those two extra months in at the beginning of the year. But I prefer the Anglo-Saxon name for the month, the Pythonesque "Blotmonath", after the festival they celebrated at this time of year when they slaughtered cattle as sacrifices to the pagan gods.

One of November's fame-claims is that it is not mentioned in any of Shakespeare's plays and, in the USA, land of crazy ideas, November the first is "National Men Make the Dinner Day". I can't imagine Donald Trump celebrating that.

***

Walking out on a winter's day when the sky is grey and all the leaves are brown reminds me of the first four lines of The Mamas and the Papas' song *California Dreamin* but, according to the next lines they had the option of retreating to sunny and warm LA whereas I'm stuck in cold and cloudy Stanwick.

1 November. The day that the leaves came down – well, many of them anyway. A drop in temperature has provided the trigger and many trees are discarding their foliage which flutters down like golden snowflakes. On path sides, there are piles of multi-browned wind driven leaves. In travelling around the area, I have noticed that the trees higher up the slopes of the Nene valley have browned quicker than those near the river in the valley bottom. I deduce that the higher ground water level down there provides more moisture for the vegetation consequently the leaves are better nourished and do not dry and wither so quickly.

New England in the USA is famed for the autumn colours of its trees but, in places, the ones in "old" England can be just as spectacular. Where trees have still retained their foliage, a colourful beauty has returned to the countryside adorning it with hues from bright lemon yellow, through golden to a dark chestnut while neighbouring stands contrast by retaining their greenness.

***

November the second and I'm still gathering walnuts. This morning we had the first frost of the winter and the temperature was only three degrees when we arrived at the Lakes at eight o'clock. There is an old rhyme;

> *If there's ice in November to bear a duck,*
> *There'll be nothing after but sludge and muck.*

So, I'm praying that the lakes don't freeze.

***

I bet when Mrs May accepts my invitation to Stanwick Lakes she brings her trekking or Nordic walking poles as I have read that walking with them is one of her favourite pastimes.

Walking with these poles is an excellent way of exercising and can help tone your physique; furthermore, it burns forty-six percent more calories than ordinary walking because, as you press down with the poles on each stride, you also exercise your arms, shoulders and chest.

I also walk with two poles but for a further reason. Being an arthritis sufferer, I find that the poles relieve pressure on my joints, particularly the back, hips and knees, and I can therefore walk further less painfully. When I first bought the poles, I could only walk about a mile and, even then, I needed to sit on every seat. Now I can manage two or three miles with no sit-downs. Also, after being unable to do so for many years, we can now go on walking holidays covering six or seven miles during a day in three steady stages.

So, my message to fellow arthritis sufferers is, don't give in to the pain, buy some trekking poles, use them daily if you can, and you will gradually increase the distance you can walk, the pain will ease with the exercise and you will rediscover enjoyment of the countryside.

8 November. There was a very heavy frost this morning and the temperature was minus three degrees when we reached the Lakes but it was a sunny, windless morning which made for very pleasant walking. Ann had so many layers of clothing on she could have been a stand-in for the Michelin man.

Some of the swan families are beginning to break up, with the parents aggressively chasing away their cygnets when they feel the youngsters can look after themselves. This usually occurs late in the year, about six months after the cygnets are born, when they have reached full size, their plumage has become predominately white and they have learnt to fly. They then join a "youngster" flock, a sort of teenage gang, while their parents stay on the breeding lake. The non-mated juveniles remain in these flocks for three or four years then they find a mate, usually from their own flock, and the two of them fly off to find their own breeding water. But it is no honeymoon because they become involved in many fights as they try to move into already occupied territories. At Stanwick Lakes, most of the lacustrine nesting sites have already been commandeered by pairs of swans and the newly arrived couples increasingly must find a home along stretches of the river.

***

One thing that annoys me at Stanwick Lakes is the amount of litter left by visitors, particularly at weekends. I can't understand how people can come to a beautiful natural location then despoil it by not considerately disposing of their rubbish.

It is especially exasperating when the litter is

discarded only a few metres from a bin but, to be fair, humans are not always the culprits in this instance. I have watched crows scavenge from the bins, pick through the contents and flick them aside with their beaks in their search for food scraps. They are clever and resourceful, and I saw one peck at the top of a tied-up plastic bag to untie the knot then open it up before probing around inside; it finally flew off with a scrap in its beak but not before it had scattered bin contents on the ground all around.

11 November. We met bird expert, Steve, this morning and he reported seeing a yellow-browed warbler; now, I have never heard of this bird, so I began to suspect Steve's imagination might be slipping into avian overdrive but I did some research and found that yellow-browed warblers are becoming increasingly common in the UK during winter. In the 1970s about seventy were recorded each year but now there are over five hundred sightings. They are very small – about the size of a goldcrest, our smallest bird, and their plumage is green above and white beneath; also, they have a distinctive pale yellow eyebrow; their call resembles that of a coal tit – a "tseeweest" sound.

These amazing minute birds must have phenomenal endurance as they make their long haul migratory flight to reach us from their breeding grounds in Asia, mainly Siberia, Mongolia and north east China.

The reason they are becoming more common here in our winter is our increasingly mild oceanic climate, which appeals to the birds because it is only (?) about three thousand five hundred kilometres from their breeding grounds whereas their traditional destination in south east Asia is about six thousand kilometres away.

***

I am being particularly vigilant when looking at trees right now because of reports in the press that the arboreal disease, ash dieback, is now spreading rapidly across the country after first being recognised in Poland in 1992.

Assuming you know your ash from your elder, ash dieback can be recognised by shrivelled black shoots on the trees and dark, long, thin diamond-shaped lesions on the trunk at the base of dead shoots. The disease is caused by the fungus blocking the trees' moisture conveyance system. The current increased concern about dieback fungus is because it has been found that it can adapt and start to kill other species including privet and lilac. Furthermore, research has shown that the disease, which it was previously believed was carried by windborne spores, can be transmitted by the spores sticking to objects such as tyres and boots. For this reason, I especially check the ash trees in the little copse next to the A45 lay-by because traffic travelling long distances stops there and could be carrying the disease.

Ash trees are extremely important because they comprise twenty percent of our woodland and they are relied on as a habitat by many species including mammals, invertebrates, insects, lichens and harmless fungi. Also, ash is one of the toughest hardwoods and is used for the handles of axes, hammers and spades as well as for hockey sticks and oars.

So, what can we do about this disease? We can learn to look out for the signs and, if we suspect any, report them to experts or, in this case, the rangers at Stanwick Lakes; they will know the measures that must be taken to eliminate or contain the infection. Finally, WE ALL NEED TO PLANT MORE TREES to provide a diverse range which can help species recover more quickly. Also, trees improve our air quality because they absorb the carbon dioxide which traps heat in the atmosphere and prevents it being released into space, the phenomenon known as the "greenhouse effect".

14 November. I'm excited today as I have another bird to add to my "second-hand" twitching list because we met Bob Webster this morning and he reported seeing a bearded tit flitting along the reeds at the side of the causeway.

The name "bearded tit" is a misnomer because, firstly, the males have a Mexican revolutionary style moustache and not a beard; the females lack the moustache. Secondly, it is not a member of the tit family but is a unique songbird not related to any other species; it is called a "tit" because of its resemblance in shape and size to a long-tailed tit. Because it frequents reed beds it is often also called a bearded reedling and usually the first clue to its presence is its metallic "ping" call. It is quite rare with only around six hundred breeding pairs in the UK.

***

Something that mystifies me in the countryside is what happens to all the carcasses of creatures when they die or are killed. At Stanwick Lakes we know there are many mammals such as munjacs, foxes, badgers and otters as well as large birds like swans and herons. Many of them have short lifespans so we ought to regularly encounter carcasses or skeletons but we rarely do.

I did some research to try and find the answer. It is believed most wild creatures instinctively become aware of their impending demise and return to their dens, lairs or resting grounds to die; otherwise, their own species drag or carry them to these locations. (Badgers have even been observed digging holes and ceremoniously burying their dead.) There they are initially consumed by scavengers such as foxes, magpies and crows, or even their own kind; foxes, in particular, are known to be cannibalistic. Next to arrive to assist in the process are the flies and beetles; these, together with insect larvae, fungi, bacteria, slugs, snails and earthworms, are the detritivores which often work together to feed on decaying matter so the nutrients are returned to the ecosystem. These are nature's recyclers and they consume the dead matter very gradually, sometimes over years, to convert it into forms used by other organisms.

Finally, only bones and hair remain and the last to play

a part are creatures like voles and mice which gnaw on the remnants to obtain calcium; this can also take many years until nothing visible remains of the deceased creatures.

***

I can't remember a year when most of the leaves have clung to their branches for so long into the autumn; they are usually shed by Guy Fawkes' night. But after two mornings of heavy frosts, storm Angus, the first of the winter, has blown in bringing strong winds with gusts of cavalry charge intensity; then the rain followed and the landscape underwent a sudden change with much of the foliage being stripped over two days.

The scene inspired me to write a pararhyme – with a little help from the Bard.

Rough winds do shake November's trees,
Denuding them of all their leaves,
Hurling branches back and forth,
Sending their clothing down to earth.
Some resist, defiant, firm,
Even so, it's soon their turn,
At last they stand naked, ungowned,
Spiky spectres 'cross the land.

I feel sadness for the loss,
But no need to feel distress,
The trees bide time, they have their plan,
'Cos deep inside new growth's begun,

Young life in sap is pushing through,
From roots to trunk to every bough,
In preparation for the spring.
November winds, you'll never win.

21 November. A polar blast has hit the country bringing snow to many areas but here we have merely had two days of persistent rain. This has caused the river water level to rise about two feet and has filled the path depressions with puddles we need to sidestep. The sky is consistently grey with just a pale wash of luminosity. As we cross the causeway into the northerly wind our faces are stung by a fusillade of near horizontal icy rain. There are very few people about and we only meet three dog walkers and three joggers.

With the colder weather and shorter hours of daylight there are noticeably less people at the Lakes but recent research has shown that it is equally important to go outdoors in winter to get enough sunlight for our bodies to create vitamin D which is needed to keep muscles, teeth and bones healthy. Also, people who exercise outdoors in winter benefit psychologically and are less likely to suffer from Seasonal Affective Disorder.

***

Some months ago, an earthworks contractor was employed at the Lakes to dig a channel between two sections of the river near the Treehouse Hide. It formed a straight line joining two points on a bend and it increased the amount of flow the river could carry to minimise the flooding of the pasture to the south and the nature reserve on the north.

Now, after several days of downpours, the channel is fully employed and a torrent is racing down it. It is partially fulfilling its purpose but the paths are already flooding and any more water flowing down the valley will reduce its effectiveness. I looked at the channel again this morning (the twenty-fifth) and, although there was water flowing through it, I think it will need to be deeper and wider before the river chooses it as its preferred course.

Dave, the ranger, informed me that another reason for digging the channel was because the strong flow of water entering the river bend was eroding the bank; therefore, it was intended that the channel would ultimately become the main river course and prevent further erosion, leaving the bend as a small oxbow lake. This bend has been known for many years as "Neddy's Bend" but it is not known who Neddy was; The only explanation I can think of is that "Neddy" is an old English word for a jackass so possibly one of these animals was once tethered there, or one of the local men who worked on the land in the valley was considered stupid so they nicknamed him after that beast.

In addition to the channel, the diggers excavated shallow pools which it is hoped will attract waders to the area near the Hide.

The entire project was achieved through funding received from the Dulverton Trust which is a grant-making charity founded by Lord Dulverton in 1949.

The two storey Treehouse Hide was officially opened in April 2014 and was built by the rangers and volunteers supported by lottery funding. It has sweeping views over the pasture meadows and a large lake with a spit of land projecting into it which is a regular haunt of unusual birds such as waders.

Whilst passing that way, we went into the Hide especially to look for the kingfishers, but their nest holes were sadly below water level and there were no signs of the homeless birds.

***

Almost every morning when we drive along the access road into the Lakes, there is a pair of magpies pecking the ground and hopping about. I can tell they are up to no goodby the way they guiltily fly up into the trees as we approach. With their arrogant attitude, they are like feral teenagers hanging around on a street corner; they have even been likened to football hooligans – presumably from Newcastle because of their strip. I don't know what attracts them to the tarmac surface because I can't see anything on which they can scavenge but it must be addictive because they soon fly down again after we pass. I presume they believe that, if they are dressed in smart black and white military style uniforms, they can get away with anything!

Magpies are one of the most resourceful and intelligent animals and their numbers have tripled over the last thirty years partially due to the increased amount of roadkill on which they scavenge.

They have an unwarranted reputation for stealing shiny objects; this false belief derives from a French play, *La Pie Voleuse,* in which a servant is accused of stealing silverware and is sentenced to death, when the thief was actually a magpie. Later Rossini used this story in his opera, *La Gazza Ladra,* and the magpie's thieving character became universally believed.

26 November. On a woodland path, we passed through two areas of olfactory haze; they only lasted a few metres and we stopped and sniffed; it was a rancid, musty yet slightly sweet smell and the nearest I can get to describing it is that it reeked of very, very sweaty unwashed feet. We looked into the undergrowth but there were no signs of any animal passing or flattening the vegetation. This was the scent of foxes marking their territory which they do with their urine and faeces and through secretions from an anal sac – either that or my feet needed washing!

29 November. It's minus five degrees and even the dog has got his coat on; as it's red, with his white fur, he looks like a miniature Santa Claus. Nature has provided him with his winter wonderland and a hoar frost is coating the ground and trees; on the causeway bridge handrail, the short frost particles stand like a white crew cut. The river temperature is warmer than that of the air and steam rises smokily from it as though from a thermal hot spring. When I raise my binoculars to my eyes I can't see anything because my hot breath mists up the lens. But it's sunny and there's little wind so it's a pleasurable, if cold, walk.

DECEMBER

It's December and again I prefer the Anglo-Saxon name for the month, Yule Monath, instead of being confused by the Roman tenth month word. Yule Monath is named after the cosy warming tradition of burning large logs in the hearth at this time of year.

***

I have now started on my chocolate advent calendar and am up to the twentieth of December already.

Earlier in the week there was a Santa Fun Run at the Lakes and hundreds of people dressed as Father Christmas jogged along the paths. This event caused me some concern because every year at the end of the autumn term I dress up and become the only, genuine REAL Santa Claus at Little Harrowden Primary School. So, I hoped none of the children from that school saw the Fun Run and became confused by all the imposters.

The annual procedure at the school is that I sit in an armchair in the library and each class, starting with the youngest and cutest, the Reception class, comes and sits on the floor at my feet. I then give them some spiel about my life as Santa Claus and ask if they have been well behaved; if they haven't, I tell them they risk being entered on my naughty list and therefore getting no, or low value, presents. Next comes the challenging part for me when I ask them if they have any questions and I have to think "on the hoof" to answer such posers as, 'How do you manage to deliver gifts to all the children in the world in one evening?' or 'How do you get into modern homes that don't have a chimney?' I usually manage to dream up some half-credible explanations but if a child probes persistently I say, 'That's enough of that subject – next question, please.' Lastly, I give them all a small gift and they leave. Then I have a few minutes to recharge my imaginative powers before the next bunch of little interrogators arrives.

Finally, it's the class of the oldest children; they no longer believe in Santa Claus; they look rather bored; they don't have any questions; they just want to get their present and get out of there.

As I watched the Fun Run participants my concerns were allayed because they were mainly slim, healthy types whereas Santa needs to be me-shaped, that is, portly, rotund and round bellied with a gruff, whisky-brown voice – *ho, ho, ho!*

On the subject of children at Christmas, I heard a snippet on Anneka Rice's radio programme; a little boy came home from school and told his parents they were going to perform a play about Mary and Joe Smith.

5 December. This morning, at Neddy's Bend, three, usually very secretive, water rails were swimming with a small flock of Canada geese. The water around the lakeside reed beds, which are the usual haunts of water rails, was frozen over causing them to venture further for their breakfast; they are timid, and scurry into the reeds when they sense our presence but the Canada geese look at us unconcerned as though wondering what all the fuss is about.

Water rails become more numerous in winter when many migrants arrive from Europe but in today's political climate, the less said about that the better.

Word has got around amongst birdwatchers about the bearded tits seen in the reed beds near the causeway; yesterday we met a man who claimed he had seen two of them and there were several people, some with telescopes, peering hopefully across the reed tops; all they could claim was that they had probably heard one.

***

Disappointingly, the replica Iron Age roundhouse[1] continues to be vandalised; the external daub coating has been knocked off in several places and there are even large holes in the wattles on either side of the entrance posts. This is very sad as the roundhouse is an important feature in making visitors aware of Stanwick Lakes' historical past. To keep the structure in a pristine condition would require ongoing maintenance from the rangers but each spring they patiently restore it; next year it will be a more major project as some of the roof beams have rotted and need replacing.

---

1   Sadly, since writing this, the roadhouse has collapsed and had to be removed.

It may be a good idea to also have, next to the roundhouse, some medieval punishment stocks so, if any of the yobs responsible for the vandalism could be caught, they could, subject to judicial approval, serve a corrective sentence there. As they say locally 'That'll larn 'em.'

6 December. In addition to our morning walk, today we also joined the Irthlingborough Cub pack for a night hike at the Lakes. I led twenty youngsters and four leaders into the gloom – torches were not allowed. I had hoped to see some nocturnal wildlife but didn't see any, partly because of the darkness, but also because they had fled from the boisterous shrieks and chattering of twenty excited children.

As I strode with my trekking poles like a sergeant major at the vanguard of a noisy column of miniature soldiers, I felt we could invade a small third world country; they would surely have surrendered on being terrified by the approaching pandemonium. But all we managed to commandeer was the play equipment near the rangers' cabin and the only casualty we suffered was a lad who had some sand flicked in his eye.

When I led the group back to the A6 gate, two Cubs walked by my side chatting to me. One of them said with profound seriousness that, in the gloom, he had seen a huge creature. I asked him how big it was and he showed me, by spreading his hands, the size of its head; I estimated it was about two feet across. This lad had obviously discovered a new species, of Bengal Tiger size, prowling around the Stanwick Lakes area – walkers beware!

8 December. A red kite flies slowly, almost hovering, across the slate grey sky; it is quartering the ground methodically scanning it like a satellite for prey. It checks its progress, wheels round and drops several metres; it has spotted some movement; it circles a few times, abandons the kill attempt and resumes its original flight path. It won't be long before it feeds as the dying vegetation has made its quarry more visible; some mouse, vole or small bird now has a limited lifespan.

Near the Visitor Centre, a kestrel is on a similar mission but he has mastered the hovering art and doesn't have to put in the miles, like the kite, to find his meal.

***

Also because of the dying vegetation, dunnocks and wrens are no longer able to creep secretly among the undergrowth and are now seen flitting from bough to bough. But there is one character which never seeks secrecy and that is the robin; they are bold, audacious and unafraid of people, and often on our walks one will appear on a branch only a few metres in front of us; it cheekily cocks its head to one side to strike a Christmas card pose then flits just a short distance away as we pass. Because these birds are territorial we often have several similar encounters on our walk. In the rhyme, he is called "cock robin" but "Cocky Robin" would be more appropriate.

The reason for the robin featuring on Christmas cards is due to a connection with Christianity. One legend relates that after the birth of Jesus, a robin fanned the flames of a fire to keep the baby warm and, in doing so, singed his breast turning it red. In another story, the red breast is explained by the bird, which was previously brown, singing to Christ on the cross to comfort him and blood from a wound dropping on the bird and staining it. Another explanation is that a robin plucked a thorn from the forehead of Jesus as he was on the way to Calvary and blood from the thorn-cut fell on the bird's breast. What wonderfully imaginative ways they had in those days of explaining the beauties of nature.

With regards the first of these legends, I think the real miracle of Jerusalem is not the Virgin Birth but that the little robin, by frantically flapping his tiny wings, could generate enough flames to heat the entire stable. He didn't become red-breasted only by being singed but by the sheer exertion of his effort.

Of course, the bird's breast is actually orange and not red but the word "orange" only came in to usage in England in the sixteenth century when the fruit was introduced; by that time the name red-breast had become universally used and remained so thereafter.

16 December. I mentioned last month the part of the river which was historically known as Neddy's Bend; whilst walking with Dave Rees this morning we passed it and he told me the Stanwick youngsters used to call it Ankle Bay, and they regularly paddled there.

This is confirmed in a quote by the Stanwick Chatterbox Group in *Memories of the Nene Valley* compiled by the Bedfordshire, Cambridgeshire and Northamptonshire Wildlife Trust.

'I remember using the river bank at Ankle Bay as a beach, learning to swim, paddling and splashing around – mums would come down and bring jam sandwiches. The water was really clear because of the gravel so the children didn't get dirty either. Lots of children had knitted costumes which would get very heavy and soggy when wet. The river was our seaside.'

***

The lapwing flocks have returned and are now seen, in great numbers, tumbling around the sky in coordinated displays. Some instinctive sense empowers them to all change direction in a nanosecond. These massed gatherings have migrated from cold areas of northern Europe to find milder conditions in the UK.

Their performance may not match the dense sculptural murmurations of starlings seen in some places but they still have us mesmerised in wonderment for several minutes.

***

The grey heron I mentioned in January has returned to his early morning winter angling pitch next to the channel between the two lakes near the Stanwick brook. Only because I expect him to be there can I distinguish his form, his greyness blending with the mist and the cloud-reflecting lake behind. He stands motionless and poised and vigilant and ready to strike.

17 December. Something has stimulated the blackbirds to be particularly active and frisky – maybe the exceptionally warm weather. They are not usually flocking birds but I saw about ten of them, in the company of redwings, hopping around and pecking at the grass near a small lake next to the car park. Males have been chasing and making advances to the females; they often lay eggs in February so this is probably the start of their courtship efforts or, at a stretch of the imagination, this heightened libido could be linked to the fact that today is the start of the Roman festival of Saturnalia. This is a seven-day orgy of eating, drinking and doing other things – rather like an extended office party. In Roman times, it was a holiday for the slaves (office workers) who were waited on by their masters (managers, directors etc.; did I hear someone say, 'fat chance').

18 December. When we met Bob Webster on the railway bridge he told us two or three bitterns had been seen lurking in the reed beds. In all the years I have been walking at the Lakes, I have only seen bitterns twice, once, early one Sunday morning, one flew up from some reeds in front of me and another time one was flying across a lake.

Bitterns are the third UK members of the *Ardeidae* family the others being grey herons and little egrets. They are secretive birds which move slowly through the waterside reeds hunting for fishes. They are difficult to see because their striated brown plumage camouflages them well in their surroundings. However, in the spring their presence is often revealed by the very loud booming call the males make to attract mates; the sound can be heard over a mile away.

There are around eighty breeding pairs in this country but in winter their numbers are swelled by migrants arriving from Europe. Due to conservation measures resident birds are increasing and it is now believed we have more than we've had for over two hundred years.

In Victorian times (those bloody Victorians again!) bitterns were a favourite target of taxidermists and, as a result, it is believed there are more bitterns in glass display cases in East Anglia than there are in the wild. This hunting caused the bird to become temporarily extinct in this country in 1886.

***

The weather is mild but it is a time of dampness and the sun doesn't have the strength or the length of time in the sky to dry the ground. This dampness has caused the growth of orange cup fungi on some dead tree trunks and logs. There is a good display of about twenty of them on a fallen trunk near the footbridge over the Stanwick brook and they bring a welcome dash of brightness to the drab winter surroundings. I am not a fungi expert but I believe these to be velvet shank fungi which are an edible mushroom although I personally wouldn't risk eating them because they often grow side by side with the deadly poisonous and similar *Galerina Marginata.*

21 December. It is still dark when we arrive at the Lakes just before eight o'clock and a weak light seeps across the land during our walk until it is fully daybreak by the time we return to the car park.

It is a joy to catch nature awakening; a large flock of house sparrows begins to chat noisily in a hedge; the first forays of lapwings call overhead; a grey squirrel scampers down from a drey. Caillou spots two rabbits on the path ahead and races after them pulling his lead out to its full stretch and dragging Ann into a jog behind him; but he is a useless and too slow hunter, and the rabbits have long gone by the time he reaches the place where he saw them disappear into the undergrowth; he stands, peers and raises his nose slightly to sniff, but the chase is over.

On the lakes, the wildfowl are difficult to identify because they are merely silhouettes against the sky-lightened water.

A flock of about fifty early rising Canada geese attempt their version of a murmuration but they are too sluggish and spread out to achieve a commendable display; their turns are slow and laboured, and they further spoil the attempt by insisting on honking loudly – a gaggle of ridiculous pantomime dames busying across the sky's stage.

***

My wife has a cold and I think I am beginning to catch it. The vicar told me that the best way to fend off a cold was to drink plenty of whisky. No, sorry! I remember now, it wasn't the vicar who told me that but the man selling *The Big Issue*.

23 December. The hazel trees are at last shedding their foliage and the large round leaves lay around the multi-stemmed trunks like yellow beer mats. They are now being replaced by the newly forming catkins which will open in the new year into the tree's long pollen-rich pendulous adornments.

25 December. This is the only day of the year when Stanwick Lakes is closed to vehicles but we regular dog-walkers are not to be denied our daily walk and several of us are parked outside the barrier on the access road. There are three cars there when we arrive but we see few people on our walk; however, those we do meet are charged with Christmas bonhomie and greet us heartily whether we know them or not.

At the end of our stroll the car park is deserted, the Visitor Centre closed, there is no-one at the rangers' cabin and no children swarming over the playground equipment. The place has an eerie, still, quiet beauty and is like a deserted village; I wonder how long it would take nature to reclaim it if it stayed that way.

***

The sights you see when you haven't got your gun – or camera! If I'd have been carrying the latter this morning instead of my new Christmas-present binoculars I could definitely have captured a competition winning photograph.

When I checked if the heron was at his usual spot, at first I couldn't see him then I noticed he was perched about four feet above the ground on a branch. As I watched, a munjac sauntered out from the bushes and stood immediately beneath the heron; they were only inches apart and both remained motionless for several seconds, their profiles standing out clearly against the lake in the background and they were seemingly unconcerned about the presence of each other. Finally, the munjac continued on his way into the shrubbery and the photo opportunity had gone forever.

28 December. Dave points out a very small bird which has flitted across the path in front of us. Initially I assume it is a wren but it obligingly poses, robin-like, on a branch as we approach and I see it is a goldcrest. It tamely escorts us for a few yards by bobbing along the lower branches as we walk on.

Goldcrests are our smallest bird being about a centimetre smaller than a wren, and Suffolk herring fishermen used to call them "tot o'er the sea" because goldcrests often landed on their boats in the North Sea. Also, it was once believed that goldcrests migrated across the sea by hitching a ride on the backs of woodcocks because the two birds arrived on the east coast at the same time and the larger woodcocks had been seen but not the much smaller goldcrests.

The land that Stanwick Lakes occupies has had many uses over the years. For most of that time, in pre-history, it would have been in the earth's unspoilt natural state with vegetation growing uncontrolled and creatures roaming freely over it. Then, in the Mesolithic period, hunter-gatherers would have fed on the edible plants and chased down the pre-historic animals.

Next, in the Neolithic period (4000 – 2500 BC), agricultural methods were introduced from the Continent leading to deforestation and humans settling more permanently in some areas to tend their crops. At that time, the British Isles was still part of continental Europe due to the Doggerland landmass which is now beneath the North Sea

Agriculture continued until this century at Stanwick Lakes mainly as pasture because frequent flooding limited its arable potential. Then, in 1985, these thousands of years of farming came to an end as most of the land became quarries for gravel extraction for use in construction. This terminated in 2004 when the land was purchased by the East Northamptonshire Council and subsequently Stanwick Lakes was created – hooray!

Now it is, what author, Robert Macfarlane in his book *Landmarks* labels "Bastard Countryside" which is land that has had an industrial use but has now been returned to nature.

So, we humans now have the opportunity to enjoy the land again, but we are merely visitors; the creatures that are the permanent residents are the true owners of Stanwick Lakes and it is appropriate that they should have the last words in this book.

***

On the last evening of the year Phil, the fox, sat in his den with his pal, Bill, the badger; they were exchanging their favourite stories about the curious things they had seen during the last twelve months.

Bill told his story.

'Once upon a time in a beautiful magical land called Stanwickia, early each morning came a race of people called the Doggie-walkie-peeps. They came, that is, as long as the Uppy-barrier elf had remembered to raise the entrance barrier.

The Doggie-walkie-peeps were transported to Stanwickia in rolling capsule creatures with yellow staring eyes. These, the lake creatures called Brum-bastards because of the disturbing noise they made as they rolled along and because several of their friends had died after being hit by them.

Once inside Stanwickia the Brum-bastards disgorged their cargo of Doggie-walkie-peeps which had, at the end of a leather thread, a little furry beast called a Poo-popper. As the Doggie-walkie-peeps walked around Stanwickia the Poo-poppers deposited droppings at various points which the Doggie-walkie-peeps treasured and lovingly gathered in little black plastic sacks. Further along the paths these sacks were fed to the greedy red rotund creatures called Bin-sloths which clung to posts like their Central American cousins attached themselves to jungle branches. These Bin-sloths hungrily devoured the offerings through their flappy black mouths and showed their appreciation by a plopping burp as they clamped their stinking orifices shut. (Phil and Bill giggled here as they had often watched this strange ritual while hiding in nearby bushes.)

Often the Doogie-walkie-peeps met and gathered chatting in small groups but Bill and Phil, hidden nearby, could never understand the noises they made.

"Bit blowy today."

"Gonna have some rain later."

"My dog seems to have a bit of diarrhoea."

Eventually, the Doogie-walkie-peeps returned to their Brum-bastards and rolled away to their Brickie-dens, and peace returned to Stanwickia.'

***

'Time for me to be going,' said Bill.

'Thanks for popping round for a chat,' said Phil.

And as Bill waddled his way back to his sett he heard a village church bell strike midnight and the year at Stanwick Lakes came to an end.